# LIGHT
## An Aut

'Light In The Dust' conveys the essence of the first 21 years of the author's life. Born in 1939 her first years were happy because of her father's absence. His demobilization ensured that Joan Mary's 'War' on the Home Front began in 1946 and outlasted her teenage years.

Only her irrepressible optimism helped her to survive. She shares the joys and fears of her early life, describing her search for wholeness in the face of great odds.

This is a story of the survival of the human spirit in the face of parental oppression and social and economic deprivation. It points to a greater need for compassionate understanding in a society often deaf and blind to the mental scarring of the growing child, and, by definition, of the adult.

Note on the author to-day. Jo Mary has just gained a B.A. in Humanities. She lives with her youngest child and her cat. Apart from being a full-time parent, she is now pursuing a writing career and researching compassionate caring approaches which may help others to experience the joy of healing and wholeness. Her main interests are gardening and child development.

# DEDICATION

For my children. The love that I bore them helped to keep me alive long enough to learn to love myself. And for Cedric, who never ceased to believe in me; In memoriam.

> *"But love me for love's sake, that evermore*
> *Thou may'st love on, through love's eternity."*

Elizabeth Barrett Browning. 1806–1861.

# DISCLAIMER

This is my story. My siblings would have told the tale differently. For this reason I have disguised family names and street names. Also, names and physical characteristics that would identify other characters in the book have been altered. Otherwise I have adhered to the truth, as I recall it, as closely as it is possible to do so within the context of writing a book.

# ACKNOWLEDGEMENTS

I would like to thank the writers Brian McCabe and Hilary Parke who patiently guided me through the first draft of this book, and Dr. Donald Low of Stirling University for his positive encouragement in seeking publication. Many thanks also to the people who supported me both emotionally and financially during the lengthy pre-publication period. Most especially I would like to thank The Society of Friends for just 'being there'.

An Autobiography by Jo Mary Stafford. *(Pen name)*

# LIGHT IN THE DUST

(Quaker author)

920

Trustline Publishing, P.O. Box 5, Crieff, Perthshire PH6 2YA.

First published 1990.

ISBN No. 0 9516438 0 0

Typeset and printed in Great Britain by Caric Press, Andover, Hants. (0264) 354887.

Distributed by Vine House Distribution, Waldenbury, North Common, Chailey, East Sussex BN8 4DR. Tel. 082 572-3398

Part One

# CHILDHOOD

| | | |
|---|---|---|
| 1. | War Was Peace | 1 |
| 2. | V. E. Day | 5 |
| 3. | The 'A' Bomb | 8 |
| 4. | The Babby's Birth | 12 |
| 5. | 1946. Poverty and Change | 19 |
| 6. | Smells | 23 |
| 7. | The Ghost of Christmas Past | 29 |
| 8. | Bath Night and Other Horrors | 33 |
| 9. | Walks in the Black Country | 38 |
| 10. | The Old Garden | 42 |
| 11. | Lost Innocence | 46 |
| 12. | Going to the Pictures | 52 |
| 13. | Children's Games | 59 |
| 14. | Paper Dolls and Other Games | 67 |
| 15. | Social Changes | 71 |
| 16. | The New Garden | 78 |
| 17. | Learning Lessons | 85 |
| 18. | Evenings at Home | 90 |
| 19. | Father's Poultry Phase | 97 |
| 20. | Religious Instruction | 101 |
| 21. | Some Neighbours | 107 |
| 22. | Signs of Womanhood | 111 |
| 23. | Last Year of Schooling | 119 |
| 24. | Fifteenth Birthday | 123 |

Part Two

# WOMANHOOD

| | | |
|---|---|---|
| 25. | First Job | 131 |
| 26. | Our House – Circa 1954 | 136 |
| 27. | First Love, Paul | 141 |
| 28. | Memories of Paul | 145 |
| 29. | Lost Virginity | 151 |
| 30. | Goodbye Paul | 156 |
| 31. | A Dance in Time | 160 |
| 32. | Second Job | 166 |
| 33. | Lawyer's Clerk | 169 |
| 34. | Man's Best Friend | 174 |
| 35. | Gentlemen Prefer Blondes | 177 |
| 36. | Wining and Dining | 180 |
| 37. | Start of the Sixties | 185 |
| 38. | Tired Unto Death | 188 |
| 39. | Goodbye to Shelley Road | 193 |
| 40. | Epilogue | 197 |
| 41. | Summing Up | 199 |

# LIST OF ILLUSTRATIONS

1.  Photograph of Joan Mary aged two                        127
2.  Photograph of Joan Mary aged seven                      128
3.  Photograph of Jo Mary (Joanne) aged seventeen           129
4.  School reports 1949 & 1953                              130

# PART ONE

# CHILDHOOD

## CHAPTER ONE

# War Was Peace.

To the majority of people in Britain 1939 brought chaos, incredible suffering, disaster and death and for six long years the constant threat of losing life, limb and loved ones. Few adults came out of this experience unscarred, mentally or physically, but for certain children the years of war-time would encompass the only peace they would ever know.

I was born in a council house in Shelley Road, on a slum-clearance estate on the outskirts of Walsall in Staffordshire. My arrival, in the early spring of 1939, started a long series of sick paternal jokes inferring that it was I, not Hitler, who had been responsible for the outbreak of hostilities that led to the Second World War.

My father was a small, extremely handsome youth with dark, wavy hair, cheeky blue eyes and sensuous lips. At twenty he was already the father of two daughters, so he ignored my arrival and consoled himself with vast quantities of beer and possibly a few ladies of easy virtue.

Like many an intelligent, uneducated youth, trapped by ignorance of birth-control into early matrimony, with equally youthful wives producing babies with monotonous and alarming regularity, life must have seemed a pretty hopeless proposition. After the war ended and he was demobbed he would use that native intelligence with appalling results on us all. He might have learned sadism from de Sade, but the local being nearer than the library I feel the 'credit' must go to the former and far more thriving pillar of our community.

Coming from a long line of cannon fodder dad, able-bodied and unemployed (and probably in a glow of alcoholically-induced patriotism) enlisted immediately. The direct result of this move, of which I only later became aware, was that he could no longer withhold the rent money for liquid refreshment, as the army sent the wife her share of her husband's pay direct. The Housing Department froze all Eviction Orders, allowing arrears to be paid off at a few pennies per week.

For the first time in her married life mom had a fixed income and she managed her finances astutely. Her tired body, exhausted by four pregnancies before she was twenty two years old, had time to recover. Although one baby had miscarried, in 1939 Rose Stafford was the mother of three daughters aged four, eighteen months and my infant self. Margaret, the eldest, was old enough to be fitted with a 'Micky Mouse' gas-mask, but mother did worry about how she would manage to wield two stirrup-pumps simultaneously to keep the two babies breathing, should gas be dropped on Shelley Road.

On our estate air-raid shelters were the exception rather than the rule, so Rose and her children just stayed in the black-out-curtained living room when the eerie sirens droned, warning of approaching German bombers. Birmingham was a mere seven miles away, a regular target, and soon the sound of aircraft would fill the night sky. Secure in the living room, huddled around mom on the shabby sofa, bathed in the mellow light of a solitary candle, we children knew no fear. For us it was storytime.

I see my mother now, her still-fresh face illumined by candle-glow, her baby son sleeping in her arms; Keith had been born when I was two years old, clearly helping to date my early memories. The last baby would not be born until 1945.

Our mother had dark brown hair which she curled each night with flat steel curlers. Her eyes were periwinkle-blue, her features small and neat. Her teeth had already begun to loosen and decay, discoloured by the liquid Iron Tonic used in those days to prevent anaemia. But to us children she was sweet and beautiful in the flickering firelight; the centre of our safe, secure world. She gave no hint of her own child-like fear. I recall no apprehension transferring itself to me.

The living room was sparsely furnished with an old three piece suite, a square table in the centre of the room and cheap lino on the floor. A sideboard and two dining chairs stood against the far wall. No pictures or photographs decorated the bare walls. The sofa, where we sat, was pulled up in front of the fireplace; a huge, black-leaded affair which occupied most of one wall. On the big hob-plate a kettle would be singing while below, in the oven, a large bread-pudding slowly cooked. Above the actual fire was an iron rack for airing clothes. A huge, brass-rimmed fireguard was securely hooked to the wall on either side of the grate, its Brasso'd goldness mirroring us in miniature. A brightly coloured hand-pegged rug lay before the fireplace. This was home.

Here we sat entranced, mother's soft, flat-vowelled Midland voice music to our ears as she regaled us with stories of her Birmingham childhood. Her maternal grand-parents had been lock-keepers, living beside the canal, and Rose had often stayed with them, helping her grandfather to open the lock-gates and making friends with the brown-skinned coal-carrying Bargees and their children. She talked of helping her grandmother to pick Dandelions and Bur-dock, to be made into wine and sold to passing trade. In my mind's eye I saw the cousins she played with and smelled the green fields and canals of her childhood. Only later did I learn what a tiny part these people had played in the drama of her own hideously foreshortened childhood.

After the war ended I do not recall ever again hearing mother's childish, merry laugh or sweet singing. Air raids, gas-masks, black-outs, dried Pom potatoes and rationed food could never dim the light of those short, peaceful years. Sometimes, with the 'planes thick overhead like a thousand beautiful shooting stars in slow-motion, mother crossed the back-garden with her precious bundles, handing us blanket-wrapped over the palings to our beloved next-door-neighbour. There we joined her children under their steel topped kitchen table, to fall sweetly asleep, lulled by the whistle of bombs, oblivious to our mothers' almost audibly-shaking limbs.

During those years our father was a handsome stranger

who visited infrequently. It was novel and exciting to watch him shaving in the morning, and I daringly called him 'Daddy-Paddy Wash-Face'. I didn't like it when he lay on the sofa, flush-faced, being sick into a bucket, nor comprehend mother's tears on these occasions. Nor did I understand the raised angry voices or know he was having an affair with another woman, in the seaside place where he was stationed for the Duration. The army had, for once, been quick to spot a raw recruit's potential, placing him in charge of Catering. He never left these shores to experience, at first hand, the horrors of battle. He had a very cushy number by any Old Campaigner's standards, a fact you would never have credited had you heard him expounding about Dunkirk and the like.

After the war ended we would know the dread sound of dad's approaching footfall on the outside path, painful hunger and biting cold, worn-out clothing and eternal, sadistic cruelty. From then on it would be 'Him' and 'Us', and burning, burning hatred for the man whose unwelcome return turned our peace into almost unendurable war.

During those few short years of war we prospered, comparatively speaking; and if we didn't grow fat we certainly grew healthy, both mentally and physically. We were a united family, vibrant and warm, cosy and content in the home our mother ran, single-handed, in peace.

Father was not much more than a lad himself and decades later I learned to replace hatred with pity. He didn't know any better; perhaps he never had a chance. Forgiving, unfortunately, is not forgetting, but neither do I forget those years when the lights went out all over Europe, yet lit my tender years. That time was an oasis in the desert of my childhood, when I played a small part in Heaven in that dreadful theatre of war.

CHAPTER TWO

# V.E. Day.

'Victory Day.' What did 'victory' mean? All I knew was that there was an unaccustomed softness in familiar neighbourly voices, as the grown-ups bustled around trestle tables set up in the middle of the 'horse road.' Everywhere red, white and blue flags and bunting festooned the cement-grey council houses. A home-made paper hat lurched drunkenly over my forehead. Everywhere was hazy and colourful through my unfocused eyes, disfigured by a squint. Probably the string had broken on my hated steel-rimmed spectacles.

A grown-up called for silence and children took it in turns to stand on the tables and 'do a turn'. A song or a dance, nothing very professional, but the participants were generously clapped and rewarded with gifts. Impatience and greed grappled with an inborn shyness and the knowledge that I might be laughed at. Greed won, as usual. Hoisted onto the table I belatedly wondered what I could do. Conscious even then of my unprepossessing appearance I tried to ingratiate myself with a winning smile. Luckily we didn't run to mirrors in our house so I had not yet realised that my front teeth were unattractively spaced. Later the squint and the gap would assume far greater importance, but at six years of age I still thought of myself as ordinary, if a little retarded. My elder sisters were repeatedly told how pretty or clever they were, but this Ugly Duckling had yet to peer into the reflecting water and realise its hideous shortcomings first hand. So I was still a swan, well, almost!

Tunelessly I sang a song I had recently learned at school, a sad, haunting ballad entitled 'A North Country Maid.' I

5

was proud of my memory when it came to songs and poems, and almost forty years later they are still intact when I take them out for an airing. I loved the clapping but my already hypercritical brain computed a lesser volume than the previous 'turns'. My prize was a filmy yellow-orange packet of transfers.

That is where that 'film' of the street party 'freezes'. The sun lightly caught the yellow-orange film and the sheer beauty took my breath away. Through the filmy wrapper I peered myopically at the glorious transformation of the mean ugly street, its shabby, work-worn, war-weary inhabitants and laughing, scrubbed children. I never wanted to stop looking at it that way, ever.

Later there were bonfires and shadowy figures of soldiers and miners lurching and weaving happily in and out of the smoke. Strong arms suddenly caught me and threw me high in the air, turning my world upside-down, the moon a silver ball at my feet. I had never been picked up by a man before and my stomach tensed with terror and delight.

The next memory of that historic day in our street, which I'm told made Mafeking Night look like a Vicar's Tea Party, was a stinging slap across my mouth, rattling my teeth. It was dark now, and I hadn't seen it coming. Slaps were an accepted part of our lives, like eating and sleeping, but usually I knew what my crime was, and had long since learned to anticipate blows with the skill of a budding boxer, ducking and weaving and riding with the punches. Mother's voice was sharp and hard. 'Don't EVER say that weard again.' Suddenly I was very tired and started to blart. Fat Aunt picked up my skinny body, roughly hoisting me across her ample shoulders. 'Mardy little bugger. 'Er's always grizzlin'. Let's tek 'er to bed, Rose. 'Er's tired out, anyroad up.'

Safely tucked up in the old iron ex-hospital cot I shared head-to-toe with brother Keith, face and hands given a quick cat-lick with an old strip of nappy, 'Gentle Jesus' mumbled sleepily, I began to turn the day's events over in my mind as mom clattered down 'the wooden hill', which, innocent of carpet or lino, was just that. It was safe to whisper. I confided in Keith that I had three whole pennies, 'all of me own'. "Ow did ya ger it, our Joanny?'

Keith propped himself up on one razor-sharp elbow (he was later to be nicknamed The Belsen Horror by father), his still baby-voice registering a mixture of envy and friendliness in anticipation of getting on the right side of me and sharing the spoils.

I pulled the rough army blanket over my head to keep the night monsters out, preparing to spend another suffocating night with only a tiny air hole, at the same time deftly avoiding Keith's toes exploring my nostrils. 'Well. Yer know Benjy Bennett as lives four doors down? Well. 'E sat me on the wall by our gate and told me to say shit for a penny. So I did. Then a crowd of soldiers cum laffing round me an' said they'd gie me two more pennies if I went and said it to our mom. So I did'.

'What does shit mean'? asked Keith sleepily.

'I don't know, but mom dain't 'alf gie me a clout! Still. Imagine . . . Threepence'.

So the day ended, safe in our cot, lulled by the street singing, comforted by the flicker of bonfires. There was so much to learn. What was war? What did the war being nearly OVER mean? Would we have bonfires every night? What did shit mean? "Night, Go' Bless, Keith'. "Night, Go' Bless, Joanny'.

## CHAPTER THREE

# The 'A' Bomb.

On this particular day it must have been raining, because we three girls were sitting on the stairs drawing. Josy was using carbon paper, carefully tracing around the head of an angelic-looking child in a magazine illustration. She had earlier been drawing caricatures of famous and infamous people, and on the step beside her lay a devastatingly accurate cartoon of dad. She was about seven years old and sat on the step below me, blonde curly head bent low over her work.

Nine years old Margaret was sitting on the very bottom step nearest the hall-door, sketching a landscape. She was not as absorbed in her work as was Josy, and I observed her sitting for long periods sucking the end of her pencil, brow furrowed, deep in thought.

My own drawing was messy, as usual. In my mind's eye I could clearly see the lovely rose I wished to illustrate, but try as I might it would not transfer to the drawing paper. From the wireless in the living room drifted the haunting 'Lily Marlene' and I ached for her, waiting for her soldier-lover at the Barracks Gate. The song was followed by a News Bulletin, and I became aware of Margaret straining to hear what was being said. Then she sighed, a long shuddering sigh.

'What yer thinkin', our Margaret? What's wrong?' She glanced up at me sadly.

'You'm too little to understand, Joanny. Yer know what I told yer. Ask no questions and yer'll learn no lies'. I began to nag and grizzle, disturbed at her obvious anxiety. She gave in.

8

'Oh. Alright. Yer'd best know, anyroad. In case. . . . They tested a big bomb. Last night. It's called an Atomic Bomb. It's the biggest bomb in the world'.

'Big as our 'ouse?' I queried, trying to imagine a size my young mind could comprehend.

'Bigger'n 'undreds of 'ouses. Nobody knows what'll 'appen. . . . It was exploded a long way away, but it could still blow all our winders in, and. . . . it might destroy the centre of gravity'.

Margaret's large blue eyes were wide with fear. I'd never seen her afraid before and I crept down the stairs to sit beside her and hold her hand. 'What's gravity, our Margaret?'

'Well. Ya can't see it but it's what keeps the furniture on the floor and stops us from flyin' out the winder and up into the sky. It's very important'.

I hurt somewhere deep in my stomach and my head felt funny. I longed for arms around me for comfort – Margaret's arms that hung loosely at her sides. 'But ya said the war was nearly over. We 'ad a party, remember? An' bonfires and everyfink. Why they 'gorra drop another bomb? Can't nobody stop it. . . .?'

'Nobody'. Margaret's tones were flat and final.

'Dear God,' I prayed silently, 'don't let it 'appen'. I didn't want to fly up into the sky, away from Shelley Road, away from the garden. Away from Keith. In my imagination I saw us children tumbling helplessly among the stars, saw our house getting smaller and smaller.

'Can ya breathe alright, up in the sky?' It was Josy who answered me, impatient as usual at my ignorance. 'Of course you can't. There's no oxygen in space. You'd just suffocate'. She didn't even look up from her drawing. Margaret sought to console me, assuming a more light-hearted tone.

'I only said it MIGHT 'appen. Anyroad up, we'll know tonight. No good worrying about things what might not 'appen. Cum on, Joanny, get on with yer drawing'. She, too, was soon engrossed in her sketch.

I crept back to my own stair and began picking the flaking plaster off the wall, my mind racing. What would it be like to suffocate up in the stars? Would it hurt? Why must people drop bombs? Why didn't Jesus stop them? Our Sunday School teacher said He could do anything – walk on water – make blind people see. Yes. It was my only chance. I ran up to our bedroom and picked up the Bible I had been given as 'First Prize for Perfect Attendance'. Its black shiny cover felt comforting under my fingers as I hugged it to my chest, eyes squeezed tightly shut the better to concentrate.

'Please God', I begged, 'don't let the gravity be broken. I promise I'll be good, forever. I'll not pinch the Babby's rusk again, nor suck 'is bottle. Nor tip 'im out of the pram again. It was an accident anyroad; I only wanted to see if the pram would balance on two wheels. I dain't mean no 'arm. Nor'll I ever tie the cat to the chair-leg, an' I'll try so 'ard to stop wetting the bed. But I've prayed and prayed about that an' I still do it in me sleep. An' I still get 'it for it. I won't tell no more lies, neither. Oh, please listen, Jesus. I don't want to die – ever'.

The rain had stopped and I could hear Margaret and Josy out in the front garden below the bedroom window. I trudged down the stairs and out of the front door making for my den. I tried to feel the force of gravity that held my feet to the ground when I walked.

Sitting in my den I felt so alone, comforting myself by picking the scabs off my knees and watching the green pus mingle with fresh blood. Margaret was always telling me not to do this, saying I would get blood poisoning and die. I thought of all the scabs I had stopped myself from picking and wondered why I'd bothered. At least I'd have died at home and not among the stars – alone. I could hear Margaret's dramatic tones issuing from her den, and knew she and Josy were lost in an imaginary world I could not inhabit. Why hadn't God made me like them?

In the dark hours of the night I lay sleepless, petrified, rigidly waiting. The wind sighed mournfully down the bedroom chimney. Sometime in the night the pain of fear and waiting grew unbearable and I tried to call out for mom. No sound came. It was just as well as dad, home on leave, would only shout at her if she dared to come to me. Lying rigid, listening to the creak of the staircase, waiting for gravity to cease, my eyes strained to glimpse the welcome light of early dawn. Morning came and gravity was still operating.

Finally I fell asleep, exhausted, older by far than I had been before Margaret had told me about the bomb, such a few short hours ago. The world would never again be a safe place.

## CHAPTER FOUR

# The Babby's Birth.

I knew our mom was poorly. Very poorly. Margaret said she had a bad headache and couldn't lift her head up off the pillow. Fat Aunt told me it was because I was 'such a naughty girl, such a mardy little bugger'. The Doctor said it was something called meningitis that mom had got. Lots of relatives came and went, talking in whispers, saying which children they would take 'if anything happened'. I knew nobody wanted me and expected it was because I was ugly and 'too brassy'. I didn't care much.

Granny Black, our mom's mom, came over from Birmingham. She was very ugly with a big fleshy nose and mean puckered toothless mouth. She carried her handbag everywhere, even to the lavatory, and fished her false teeth out of its depths when she ate. She hardly ever visited and always made mom cry when she did. I hated her.

She took Keith and myself to Great Barr, on the bus, and on the long walk from the bus-stop to her house she didn't even hold my hand. But then she didn't hold Keith's hand either, and he was only three. It seemed miles and miles and Keith cried to be picked up until Granny Black slapped him hard on his legs. I tried to give him a piggy-back but he was too heavy. We both ended up grizzling.

Both Keith and I were covered in itchy lumps that mom said were 'heat spots'. Mine turned to scabs when I scratched the tops off but Keith's turned to water blisters. As soon as we got to gran's house she sat him on the kitchen table and pricked them all with a needle. I hear his screams yet.

Every morning she shut him in the dark cupboard under

the stairs with his potty and refused to let him out until he'd 'done his business', or until she heard grandad's footsteps in the entry. He was an Air Raid Warden and was on Night Duty. I hated him, too. He was bald and wore steel-rimmed glasses and enjoyed feeling my knickers to 'see if I was wet'.

After tea we were shut in the spare bedroom with a chamber-pot covered in flowers, sleeping together in a musty-smelling bed. There were dark shapes and shadows everywhere. An old sofa dribbled horsehair from big rips and all sorts of junk littered the room. But worst of all were the pictures hanging from the picture rail. Big photographs of people staring at me no matter where I moved around the room. The largest photograph was of my mother's soldier brother, recently deceased. He was glassy-eyed and stiff and I desperately wanted to escape from his fearful presence.

Gran had pulled the black-out curtains across to darken the room, but I dared to open them a little and let in the sunlight. Keith and I were then able to amuse ourselves watching our headlice crawl and jump across the pillow. Our peels of laughter brought gran running upstairs to clout us both. Then Keith sobbed himself to sleep beside me, crying for his mom. I lay awake for hours in the stuffy room, too terrified to sleep.

In the morning I had tummy ache after breakfast and rushed to the toilet, too late to lift my nightie quickly enough and fouling the hem. Shaking with terror I tried to wash it at the sink but gran caught me and started beating me, knocking my head against the washbasin and calling me a 'dirty little bugger'. I thought she'd never stop hitting me.

Later that day I stood in the fussy front parlour with nothing to play with, bored and angry. The rain poured down the window. Keith slept on the chaise-longue beside the empty fireplace. All the furniture was large and covered with black shiny stuff. I stared out of the window, watching rivulets of rain race each other down the dusty panes. Gran bustled into the room to get something from the sideboard. My anger burst somewhere inside me and I felt icily calm and deadly determined.

'I 'ate ya, gran. You'm cruel. If I'd got the bus fare I'd goo 'ome and tek our Keith wi' me'.

I felt better now I'd said it. I knew what was coming without looking behind me and tried to duck. She grabbed me by the hair and dragged me into the kitchen so my screams wouldn't waken my brother, then she and grandad beat me around the room. Their evil faces told me I was in Hell. When they'd finished I dragged myself past Keith and up to the bedroom. I wished I was dead. I ached everywhere and there was a funny noise in one of my ears. My ribs hurt when I breathed so I tried not to, but it was worse when I held my breath.

Lying on the bed I turned the events over in my mind. My grandparents, I now knew, were not the cosy, kind sort of people that Margaret told us about in 'Little Red Riding Hood' or 'The Match Girl'. I did not yet know of my mother's repeated raping by her father, during her mother's many absences from home. I still cannot imagine what it must have been like for my mother, lying at home sick and helpless, knowing that I was at their mercy.

I do not know how long we stayed there. Maybe only a few days but it seemed like eternity. I do not recall the walk back to the bus stop but I do recall seeing barrage balloons suspended in the sky. Standing at the bus stop I was fascinated by the spectacle of a bomb-ruined house behind us. One wall of the house still stood, showing fireplaces and pretty wallpaper, and there was a huge crater in the front garden.

Mom's headache had gone but she was often not well. She developed a form of rheumatics in her arms and legs and had to sit on a chair at the sink to peel the potatoes. I noticed she was crying and asked what was wrong. She pushed her straggly hair out of her eyes with the back of her hand. 'Goo and play, there's a good gel. There ain't nothin' ya can do. I'll be better soon'. She was twenty five years old, had four children under nine and soon there would be another mouth to feed.

The day the baby was born mom was rushed to hospital. A neighbour sent for Fat Aunt and kept an eye on us until she arrived. Josy and I were taken to Granny Stafford's, dad's mother. Margaret and Keith stayed with Granny Black, but here Margaret would be safe and would be able to look after Keith. Granny Black favoured our Margaret, giving her lovely presents at birthdays and Christmas.

Granny Stafford was the reverse of cuddly, even though she was very obese. A formidably intelligent lady, denied formal education, she had sought to educate herself with library books. Married young she had borne twelve children of whom ten survived to adulthood. These children had been reared in a tiny terraced house, and every one of them escaped the slums except dad. Granny Stafford was dour and unapproachable, and looking back I think that she was bitter about the hand Fate had dealt her, and particularly about the husband nature had decreed for her.

Grandad Stafford was a tiny, seemingly inoffensive man with a permanently hurt expression, a Stan Laurel look-alike. A plasterer by trade, he was often unemployed and spent a lot of time hanging around the pubs he knew his sons frequented. They willingly doled out beer and cigarettes and granny despised him for cadging in this manner. She was utterly proud and would never have accepted any handout. It was a permanent puzzle to me how grandpa had managed to sire so many children with grandma. It still is.

Grandpa lived in mortal terror of his wife and sought to be invisible when she was around. Gran only spoke to him to issue orders.

''Arry, Ger out that bloody chair an' get sum coal in. Fire wants mekkin up.'

Without a word of protest or a moment's hesitation he obeyed.

'An' put kettle on while yow'm at it,' she would call contemptuously after his retreating figure. I once witnessed gran openly assaulting her husband. He was sitting on a dining chair by the fire and she, needing something from the wall-cupboard just behind him, forced her bulk through the small gap between him and the wall. He went flying. Not a word was said by either of them. Grandpa had survived every major offensive on the Somme, but none of those battles could possibly have compared, in terms of sheer torture and misery, to his later years with his wife.

Margaret was the only grandchild in our family that Granny Stafford had time for, insisting she was the only one that took after her side of the family. She constantly bragged about our better-off cousins, how well they were doing in piano competitions, or at school exams. I loathed these cousins whose hand-me-down garments I must wear. We were definitely the poor relations.

Josy and I were enrolled in the local Primary School where I made friends with a little girl improbably called Egypt. We sang 'Bobby Shaftoe' in Assembly, and I longed for a pair of shoes with silver buckles. I loved this school, doing well in lessons because the teachers were kind.

A canal ran along the bottom of the garden and here we spent hours sailing paper boats, skimming stones and watching the barges go by. Josy was always accompanied by a tiny celluloid doll bedded in a match-box, that she carried in her apron pocket. It was called Angelica. I begged and begged to have a hold of this doll, but Josy would never let me. One day I snatched it from her pocket and flung it into the middle of the canal. Josy half-killed me but I didn't care. I never did. Not on the surface, anyroad.

One Sunday our snooty Aunt Jane visited with her darling son, Clement. He joined us on the tow-path all poshed up in his Sunday best. We had on our Sunday best too, but his was much finer than ours. Clement was a real Little Lord Fauntleroy in his black velvet suit, snow-white knee-socks and black, patent leather shoes. He and lady-like Josy were soon deep in la-di-da conversation and wouldn't play with me, no matter how I begged. Prancing about on the canal bank like a Red Indian, brandishing an imaginary tomahawk, still I failed to attract their attention. I tried sticking my tongue out and making horrid faces, but still they ignored me. I was fed up and bored so I made mud balls and pelted them both with my messy missiles. Clement reacted predictably by running blarting to his dear mother, his lovely suit ruined.

Put to bed after a sharp slap from gran, I wondered what made me misbehave so and why I couldn't behave like other nice children. Josy constantly told me that I was a 'pathetic idiot'. I decided she was probably right.

On the whole I quite liked staying with Granny Stafford but was terrified of the outside lavvy. It had a big wooden seat, below which was a big hole going right down into the ground. Josy had told me that there were water rats as big as dogs living down the hole, and I just KNEW they'd jump up and bite my bottom. When I sat perched high on the seat, legs dangling above the ground, I could feel the rats getting closer, hear them coming up the hole. Screaming blue murder I would run back indoors without completing my mission.

Constipation became a problem and I was dosed with Syrup of Figs. Soon I was dashing backwards and forwards in a frenzy of fear, never stopping, as did Josy, to read the torn squares of newspaper that hung on a nail from the lavatory wall.

Finally we returned home and were disappointed to find that the new baby was not there. Margaret told us he was still in hospital and had been born very ill. When he was strong enough to leave hospital, Granny Stafford took him to her house for some weeks until mom was well enough to care for him.

Mom was lying downstairs in the big bed, which had been brought down to the living room. She looked pale and ill, and Margaret told us we must be very well behaved for her as she had had her tummy cut right open, and then sewn back up. She was a long time getting better; maybe she never did fully recover. Later I understood that she had had her last baby, having had to undergo an emergency sterilisation operation.

I was in my thirties before an elderly aunt on my father's side, who was then dying, finally put the pieces of the jig-saw together. She had been a nurse and explained that both the meningitis and rheumatics were symptomatic of the Venereal Disease mother must have been innocently suffering from for up to two years before the Babby's birth. When the baby was born the midwife discovered the mess inside her, the baby all but dead, pus oozing from his eyes. Only newly-discovered drugs saved his sight, and probably his life.

Poor mom. She knew the gossipy midwife would have told all the neighbours what was wrong. Was this, then, when she began to be a recluse? Did the meningitis cause brain damage that could help account for her changing from the happy singing mother of war-time, into a sort of helpless zombie devoid of will-power?

Father gave his mother to believe that it was his wife, not himself, who had first contracted the disease. Yet Gran Stafford herself wrote to his C.O. who put him on a Charge. Privately she continued to maintain that mother was the guilty party. When years later I tried to tell gran how her son treated me she appeared not to believe me. To her we were the slum children of a loose-moralled mother; except Margaret of course, but then she took after the Staffords.

CHAPTER FIVE

# After 1946. Poverty & Change.

Ours was a strange sort of poverty and it took me quite a while to grasp it in all its complexity. During the war years I had known we were poor, but so was everyone else on our estate. After his demob in 1946 father instilled into us the fact that we were 'better' than our neighbours. More genteel.

Our house was on the corner of the Greenpark Estate, most of whose residents were hand-picked by the Council for their general squalor. On our side, that was. The whole estate was separated into two parts by Brookspill Road, a busy main road linking Walsall and Birmingham. The 'other' side of the estate was quite posh, with hardly a single garden gate hanging off its hinges, and after the war neat wooden garages soon began to attach themselves to the houses.

Our Infant School was 'over there' and as I trudged to school, I daily marvelled at the well-kept gardens and gaily-painted woodwork. Some houses even had names. Such class. And the lady occupants didn't, as on our side of the estate, lean over their garden gates 'canting'. Stout arms folded across business-like bosoms, steel curlers poking haphazardly from turbans, coruscating as heads nodded or shook. Much tut-tutting went on, bare gums now folded in grim disapproval or scarce yellow fangs bared in shrieks of laughter at some ribald jest. And, I later realised, a lot of these women on 'our side' were only about the same age as my mother, still in her mid-twenties with a family of five. Our near-neighbours' dress was usually a shapeless smock or fold-over pinafore, the better to accommodate annual

19

changes in figure that owed nothing to their meagre diet.

I realised early in life that, whilst 'our' side of the estate was much friendlier and warmer than the 'school' side, our family would have fitted better 'over there,' because of dad. We had been so innocently at peace during the war years that dad's demobilization ushered in a shocking new era, a beginning if you like of a family cold war. Dad brought confusion and chaos to our ordered existence and a new set of rules had to be learned, fast, in order to placate the Enemy. Mother was no longer the undisputed head of the family, disciplining us with a rough but kindly hand. Now began the Rule of Terror in Shelley Road, and a colder kind of poverty blighted our lives.

There had been a great deal of neighbourly sharing during the war. After all most of the men were away at the Front, leaving the women to pull together in the common cause of survival. Red Cross Ladies paid regular visits, cheering our lives with their bright smiles and la–di–da voices, bringing layettes, bedding and many such luxuries. Now all that was over.

Father had been singled out by the Army as promising admin. material, having a superb mathematical brain hitherto unrecognised. And he could delegate. As a Regular Soldier (rather than a conscripted one) he had quickly risen to the heady rank of Sergeant, was given a cushy number on the 'home front', and garnered quite a few perks in the process. Now, demobilized and missing barking orders to his subordinates, he chose to run our 'barracks' on army lines. In clipped, semi-cultured accents, foreign to our native Black Country ears (and his own), he issued his commands.

'From now on' he told us as he lined us up for Inspection, shoulders back, tummies in, feet straight, heads up. 'This Unit will cease to be run in the old slip-shod way!' His orders, he commanded, were to be scrupulously obeyed. Rosters would be drawn up regarding dish-washing and potato peeling, coal-carrying and floor-polishing, shopping and gardening, window cleaning and darning. There was to be NO fraternising with the enemy (all our erst-while neighbours and friends). They were not, he said, 'our sort', and now he was home to care for his family we must not stoop to mother's former social level.

No more gossiping over fences for her, or nipping in and out of houses. NO-ONE would be allowed in our barracks. Also, our table manners would never pass muster in the mess and must be polished up, forthwith. Our deportment was slack, hygiene abysmal, accents deplorable. This WOULD NOT DO!

When he had finished addressing 'The Squaddies' he bade us 'Fall Out', and as I slunk away I noticed, with dreadful apprehension, the stout leather army-belt lying innocently across the table before him. And in that moment a chill entered my six-year-old soul that has taken almost four decades to banish.

In later talks he told us that he was now an 'important administrator' in the City (Birmingham), and we must collectively realise that this exalted position depended on us not mixing with the 'local peasantry', most of whose fathers were steelworkers, miners, or tubercular.

However we soon realised that, in money terms, we were far worse off than those 'peasants', because their fathers usually handed over their pay-packets unopened to their mothers. Our former playmates now boasted of cream cakes, fancy hair ribbons, new shoes and annual holidays, even if for the poorer ones the holidays consisted only of hop-picking. How I envied them their 'peasantry'. We were now reduced to abject poverty, surviving on the miniscule sum father gave our mom. Hunger and cold are relative. Combine them, however, with illness and loss of hope, and they eat into you. I dare not remember too much. I want to forget. To forgive. One must forgive, in maturity, if one is to survive and re-make a whole adult out of the fractured child.

Our father earned pretty good money, but as a 'gentleman of the City' he must dress accordingly. Hand-made shoes for his fallen arches, Crombie overcoats, Meerschaum pipes, kid gloves, tailored suits, and taxis to and from his clubs and better-class pubs. Also, he had developed a beer-gut in the army with a thirst to match. He must eat in the 'right places' whilst mother shed hopeless tears over pigs' trotters, desperately trying to make them appetising for five hungry children with rapidly-shrinking stomachs. At first she made valiant efforts, fought every bit as bravely as she had during those six long years when she had brought up her babbies single-handed, scurrying between living room, coal-house and next-door's table during air-raids, grappling with gas masks and ration books, making tasty meals out of dried egg and spam. Always she had had her finances in order. But her sacrifices for us during those years had sapped her fragile strength, and now father threatened to quench her bright child-like spirit forever.

Poverty now, while father wined and dined late into the night, meant our never being able to afford a light on the landing or in the bedroom, nightmare conditions for children grown imaginative and fearful. Whilst downstairs, mom sat in the dark until just before 'he' came home, saving the precious brightness for him. Otherwise he would be scathing about her inability to manage her finances on the 'good money' he gave her. So a precious penny must be saved each night to light him to bed. It was the same with the coal; we had to huddle shivering around a tiny flicker of flame so that a bright fire could burn for 'him'.

Each morning the ashes were sieved and every tiny re-usable scrap saved. Poverty was Keith and I picking cinders from the slagheaps behind our house near the steel works, fingers an agony of chilblains, bare legs numb. (But dad must never know else we'd get the belt for showing him up). Or Keith and I, surreptitiously kept off school, trudging three miles through snow to a canal wharf with a derelict bicycle, to return staggering, a half-hundredweight of coal slung unsteadily across the frame. Our two older sisters were too bright to miss school but Keith and I were obviously not going anywhere. We became skilled in evading the School Board man.

Later it would be the Babbie's turn, but for a little while longer we conspired to protect his childhood. Our thin hand-me-down coats were patched and threadbare, gloves a luxury we could not afford, although mom could some-times lay her hands on an old pair of socks for mittens. Keith and I were so undernourished and sickly that, at one stage, we were taken to the School Clinic for sun-ray treatment. I remember the feeling of importance as I was made to put on the requisite sun glasses before lying on the lovely warm bed. We were also given extra vitamins, free. There were then no nosey parker Social Workers to question our bruises or circumstances.

At seven dad paid for me to be admitted to a private ward of the Wolverhampton Eye Hospital, for the surgical correction of my squint. He sent his Secretary along with flowers and fruit for me and the nurses or visited like royalty, every ounce the caring middle class father, commanding admiration and respect wherever he went, scattering charm and superior smiles like confetti. While I am eternally grateful for that operation, sparing me more years of disfigurement and mockery, I am sure my father's motives were questionable. People like him just didn't have physically defective children.

Will I ever understand his motives for reading us 'The Scourge of the Swastika' whilst little more than babies, ordering us to look long and hard at the explicit photographs of naked, obscene bodies piled in open mass graves? Why did he read aloud fiction that I can recall to this day, about a man named Roderick lying gurgling with his throat cut beside his wife, while some nameless Thing crawled through a window? I will not lift the curtain further or try to recall more.

What pleasure did he get from making his younger, sturdier son box his older, puny brother, making the younger one punch harder and harder until they both cried? One from pain, the other from shame. What bitter twisted thoughts churned in his head as he surveyed his five encumbrances and his prematurely—aged, toothless, more than down-at-heel wife?

He was still young, handsome, virile, clever and desperate to better himself. In that sea-side place during the war he had met and wooed a girl who was far more fitted to him and his needs, but he gave her up and dutifully returned to us, and we gave up our childhood forever. Later, when I learned the details from old letters hidden not too well, saw the outpourings of his heart, felt the pain of his lack of fulfilment and despair, I wished he had taken his chances for all our sakes. Now he is an old man, waiting to die, alienated from most of his children by his own will and actions. I grieve for him, for the father I never knew. Maybe one day, before it is too late, he will say with true sorrow 'Forgive me, Joan' and I will answer truthfully 'It's O.K. dad. It is past'. Everything passes. But in our hearts we both know that day will never come. Not in this world, anyway.

CHAPTER SIX

# Smells.

Smells, so evocative of an age now as remote, for me, as the Ice Age. My earliest 'smell' memory is that of regurgitated beer as it spewed in a liquid-gold stream from father's mouth. And the sound as it spurted into the enamel pail placed beside the sofa, or spattered on the polished lino-leum. This memory must have been from early war-time, before he built up a tolerance to the vast quantities of beer which turned his neat figure into a strong semblance of an animated beer barrel. Today, even the remotest whiff of a brewery conjures up these memories unbidden.

But, for my fastidious nostrils, the all-pervading stench of stale urine was the most unpleasant, and I was the most persistent of the family's bed-wetters. Until the age of eleven or so I hardly knew a dry night, and my horse-hair mattress never got the chance to dry out properly. There was no extra bedding most of which, in winter, consisted of old army overcoats and such-like, and the threadbare sheets were only washed once a week on Monday morning, to be aired and back on the beds that night.

Both my brothers were incontinent, too, and the overall aroma was enhanced (if that is the right word) by the enamel bucket in our parents' bedroom, which served as a com-munal toilet during the hours of darkness. Unfortunately my mother had no sense of smell so she did not appreciate the need for constant airing of the bedrooms. The smell seeped into the plastered walls and bare floor-boards until, with time, it became an almost physical presence.

In winter or in wet weather the ground floor of our house was pervaded by steam, and the smell of singeing from clothes draped around the fireguard in the living room. Mingled with these smells was that of Zebra black lead, Mansion polish, and Snowfire ointment warming on the hob waiting to annoint our persistent chilblains. On Friday nights after our weekly bath and hair wash, I recall the smells of Lethane (an evil smelling concoction for the elimination of head lice) and Derbac Coal-Tar soap.

There was the smell of burning soot as mother illegally and persistently fired the chimney to avoid the cost of a chimney sweep, or singeing newspapers as she drew the fire when it was almost 'douted'. There was also the distinctive smell of escaping coal gas when the flame had been put out by washing boiling over on the stove.

When we were very young, before mother 'gave her neck', before she was reduced to the hollow-eyed, shuffling, walking-dead woman finally driven to near madness, there was the delicious smell of baking from scones and great trays of bread pudding bubbling in the oven beside the fire. She would spread Windolene on sparkling panes and Mansion-polish the furniture. There was Persil on washday and green bars of Sunlight soap for scrubbing the concrete kitchen floor and larder, her clear sweet voice soaring in song as she worked, before father broke her wings and silenced her sweet song forever.

There was the comforting smell of Dog's fur, innocent of shampoo, and her annual litter of ten puppies, to be tearfully sold or given away, adding their special puddle smell. And Tom Cat, fur singeing at the hob. . . . The tiny living room we called 'the house' seems almost to explode with such a profusion of remembered smells.

My delicate senses were affronted by father's constant, volcanic, anal eruptions, which my young brothers soon learned to emulate and of which father was extraordinarily proud. And in a deodorant-free age the smell of stale sweat enveloped most adults like an invisible cloud.

Mothballs! Now there's a rare, memory-provoking name and smell, conjuring up Sunday Best Clothes (in fact Sunday reeked of mothballs everywhere), and rare stately visits from elderly relatives, from the far-flung family outposts around Birmingham. Dressed in black-buttoned creaking boots and heavy black serge from top-to-toe (male and female alike) they swooped like arthritic crows, to the amazement of urchin neighbours and the acute embarrassment of my siblings and myself.

The best smells were out of doors, transporting me to realms far far away from Shelley Road. I was perhaps six when I first discovered The Rose. Rambling haphazardly and hardily in a near-neighbour's garden, conveniently near the gate, the bush cascaded and drooped with the weight of glorious milky-pinky-creamy tea roses. How long or how often I stood breathing in the heavenly fragrance I know not, but I do know that the rose represented one of my first escape routes from home, to a deep spiritual plane: a world unsullied and serene.

My fingers itched to take an armful of roses but my strict upbringing forbade me. Only once did I succumb, taking just one rose. Romantic elder sister Margaret told me we could make Rose Perfume, and together we crushed the petals and placed them in a jam-jar filled with water. In my mind's eye I saw silver-stoppered bottles of Rose Essence capturing for all time that glorious scent, to be delicately inhaled during my frequent 'Dark Nights of the Soul', when my spirit raged against poverty, ugliness and pain. But the petals turned brown and became just an evil-smelling pulp. I remembered this when, years later, I became acquainted with the lines "Lilies that fester smell far worse than weeds. . . ."

Dominating the sky-line, in one direction, were the massive cooling towers and gas-works, steaming endlessly, while in the opposite direction lay the Sewage Farm and railway junction. On hot days the sun filtered through the sulphurous haze, heating the untreated sewage. On such days the black tar ran in delightful puddles in the 'horse road', combining with the horse-dung deposited by the coal, bread and milk roundsmens' horses, providing hours of entertainment for us children as we stirred the gooey substances with twigs. An enterprising boy I greatly envied would appear at frequent intervals with barrow and shovel to scoop up the dung, selling it to local gardeners. The same lad collected potato peelings and other scraps to sell to the many illicit pig-owners. He grew up to be a very successful businessman.

Danger beckoned early for Keith and myself as we daily risked polio, diptheria, scarlet fever and many such deadly diseases that were rife in those days. We longed for some illness that would reduce us to interesting invalids and keep us from school, spending hours fishing in the forbidden drains at the side of our road. With sticks and bent pins we fished for coins dropped through the grating by unsteady late-night revellers, suffering little more than jammed skinny arms. We were both afflicted with permanent catarrh, unsavoury specimens with encrusted patches on our right sleeves, much to the disgust of our sisters, but we had the combined constitutions of a pair of oxen. Our lady-like sisters scorned our gutter games, yet they both spent weeks on end away from school with impetigo, yellow jaundice, pneumonia and such-like, drearily bemoaning their fate at missing beloved lessons and teachers. Keith and I learned early the seeming injustice of life.

The dominant smells of school were chalk, communal toilets, sweaty-foot-smelling gymnasiums and elderly teachers with B.O. The playground smelled of tar and dust, and towards lunch-time Keith and I were like Bisto Kids scenting the air for clues of delights to come from the Canteen. Permanently ravenous, our mother heading the league in Unimaginative Cooks, we adored school dinners. Lumpy potatoes, meat and vegetables, would be golluped down at record speed so we could be first in the Pudding Queue, and so first for 'seconds' and 'thirds'. Rice Pudding, frog-spawn Tapioca, Jam or Treacle Tart, Custard, Roly-Poly Pudding or Spotted Dick. Delicious, filling, ambrosial.

To us children, of necessity starved of sweets during wartime and afterwards because of poverty, school puddings were life-savers. We must have been among the first real beneficiaries of the Welfare State, an irony this as our father was a red-hot Conservative and loathed Aneurin Bevan and his ilk. Life was a paradox. It still is.

## CHAPTER SEVEN

# The Ghost of Christmas Past.

Being the eldest of the family Margaret took our infant Christmases in hand as soon as she was able. Staying up late to fill stockings was no hardship, as it was she who had kept mother company during the dark watches of the war-years, helping from late baby-hood to transport the babbies to places of comparative safety during the air-raids. She was a romantic distant child, a weaver of dreams. Whilst mom minded the house it was she who shopped for the cheapest cuts of meat, walking the two miles into Walsall to the market place each Saturday for the basic necessities. There she would scavenge for bruised fruit and vegetables, at the end of the stall-holders' day.

One particular Christmas Eve, just after the war, found Margaret as usual at Walsall Market clutching her precious pennies, her tiny face pinched with cold. Her eyes gleamed as she sought for bargains for the babbies' stockings. With bits of tinsel, frayed ribbon-ends and tissue paper that in those days wrapped individual oranges and soft fruit, Margaret could wrap a gift more beautifully than Harrods. Tortoiseshell combs, tiny mirrors, rubbers, pencils, crayons, chocolate; and always a precious tangerine for the toe of each stocking. Perhaps a cheap soft toy or dented tin drum, if she had managed to stretch the finances that far.

The Naptha flares over each stall cast a romantic glow, illuminating the frozen rosy faces of the vendors as they hoarsely cried their wares. 'Cum on. Let's be 'aving ya. Oy'll be givin' um away in a minnit. 'Ows about a noyce bunch o' flowers for the Missis? Or a pair of frilly knickers to goo with 'um . . .' Ribald cackling and much coarse comment would have offended Margaret's already lady-like sensibilities, but she paid no heed, our tiny Santa busily scurrying to and fro on her mission of magic.

The bells atop the market place carolled out their seasonal song and a soft covering of snow transformed the harsh, grimy landscape. The numerous public houses beckoned unwary travellers with welcoming arms, men and women seeking blessed oblivion on this blessed night. Drink was cheap and children numerous for most of the harassed and hopeless parents. Ragged children, blue with cold, sat on the steps of the hostelries clutching bags of 'scratchings' or penny bottles of lemonade as they settled down for the long wait until closing time.

On this particular Christmas Eve Margaret suddenly gathered her courage and made so bold as to accost dad as he emerged, unsteadily, from one of the better-class pubs adjacent to the Market place. ''Ello dad. Fancy seein' you 'ere'.

'Oh, hello Margaret my child. What on earth are you doing away from home on a night like this. You should be tucked up in your nice warm bed'.

'Yes, I'm just goin' dad. But just a second. Cum and see these oranges. . .'.

A lost man to a woman's wiles, especially one as soft and persuasive as Margaret at that moment, he followed her like the proverbial lamb. Later, weighed down with turkey, Christmas tree, holly, crackers, presents, Margaret was dispatched home in a taxi, leaving dad to continue his night's carousing with a lighter conscience and wallet.

Christmas Day proper found a scene in our house that would have done credit to a Dickens novel. Our shabby, bare living room was transformed with tinsel-decked tree, trimmings festooning every niche and patch of peeling plaster, holly hanging from the bare light bulb. The living room table, extra leaves pulled out the better to accommo-date us and the feast, groaned beneath the gigantic turkey, roast potatoes, stuffing and all, together with a huge Christmas Pudding patiently awaiting its brandied flames. The youngest children propped with pillows, there we sat pulling crackers, one ear cocked to the siren call of our shiny new toys which lay temporarily abandoned around the dusty, pegged hearth rug.

Dad, who had cooked the feast and was now carving the turkey at the head of the table, was attempting to give a fair impersonation of the genial benevolent father, while opposite him, cowering self-consciously, sat his lady-wife giving a more than fair impression of sheer misery. Margaret had been up since dawn working on mother, visions of loveliness dancing in her head, but even her genius was unequal to the task in hand.

Wide-eyed we all surveyed her handiwork. Mother's prematurely-greying hair had been crimped, singed and teased into an unbecoming haphazard mess of curls. Her pale, hollow cheeks glowed with clown-patches of rouge, her almost toothless mouth encircled with crimson lipstick applied with an extremely unskilled hand. We littler ones stared in silent disbelief at this stranger in our midst, beholding in horror THE DRESS.

Dad's most expensive Christmas present to mom was a Cocktail Dress, all gathers and flounces and flowing crêpe in an unbecoming shade of yellow-ochre. It was heavily bedecked with sequins, especially around the daring neckline which drooped unattractively over mother's sagging breasts and scarecrow-thin shoulders. God alone knows what visions had danced before father's eyes when he chose that dress, but oh! the sober light of day glared cruelly upon the scene, mother adding, with silent tears coursing down her cheeks, the final poignant touch.

Margaret, blinkered by a kindly deity, unhappily chose this moment to present to mother the final present from father, the 'pièce-de-resistance'. Unwrapped, it revealed itself to be a highly coloured wall-plaque of large proportions, depicting a Tudor-type cottage perched above a riotously-flowering cottage garden, which in turn dropped steeply to a glassy, peaceful, azure lake upon which a few swans gently took their ease. And as we stared, I swear that even the youngest of the children was aware that that heavenly scene was impossibly distant and belonged to another world entirely.

So many Christmases have passed since then, but no

magic I have since conjured up, out of much more promising material, could ever compete with Margaret's efforts. And never do the bells peel out on Christmas Even without memory firmly holding the door on that unique and extraordinary Christmas.

## CHAPTER EIGHT

# Bath-night & other Horrors.

Friday night was bath-night. On very cold winter nights mom would light the fire underneath the washing-boiler in the corner of the 'back-kitchen', to warm the water in the boiler; then she would let the fire go out and dunk us in there, one at a time, the others waiting their turn in front of the gas stove. This also happened during the dreadful winter of 1947 when there was no coal to light the living room fire to heat water for the bath. Mom hauled the settee into the tiny kitchen, where we sat toasting our toes before the stove. There wasn't room to swing a cat but we were cosy.

Most weekday nights mom washed us in front of the living room fire, sitting us one at a time on the table. We had a portable wash-stand that held a crock bowl of soapy water. That same bowl was used for mixing ingredients for baking, during the war and just after, until mother 'gave her neck'.

Most Friday nights, however, we used the 'big' bath. We girls were washed three at a time, Keith inheriting our mucky water in splendid solitude until the Babby arrived. Mom hadn't much patience or time to play with us, and I earned plenty of sharp slaps on wet arms and legs for fooling about. Being extraordinarily ticklish I squirmed with agonised laughter when mom washed my neck. 'Joan, KEEP STILL' (slap) 'Joan, I won't tell ya again' (slap).

'I can't 'elp it, mom. Really I can't'.

'Well, yer'll 'ave to 'elp it' (slap). Keith never got slapped if he laughed when mom washed him. It wasn't fair, but it was no good saying so. I'd only get another pasting.

Hair was washed in the bath with Derbac soap, smelling

33

of coal-tar, that stung the eyes cruelly. The flannel was an old bit of nappy which I liked to smell and suck. Another thing I really liked was blowing bubbles. First we soaped our hands and then blew through our half-closed fists. If one was careful, and blew gently, one achieved a huge, rainbow-hued bubble reflecting a distorted picture, in miniature, of us children in the bath. It was magic.

Lifted out of the deep iron bath we 'tazzed' through to the living room to kneel before the fire, to be roughly rubbed dry with one of the two threadbare towels the family possessed. More pain as hair was tugged at its roots. More slaps for crying. 'Joan, you'm the mardiest little bugger I ever 'ad. Shut up ya grizzling. You'm worse than the Babby'.

'Yes', I thought, rebelliously 'but when ya dry 'im ya don't be so rough AND ya sit 'im on yer knee. AND ya sing to 'im. I wouldn't be so mardy if ya cuddled me and sang 'You are my Sunshine' to me'. The Green-eyed God of jealousy was my constant companion in those days before I came to love our Keith, and later the Babby.

Poor mom, there was precious little time or energy left over from the hard grind of unremitting poverty. Vests, knickers, Liberty bodices and socks must be washed out on Friday nights, hand-wrung, and hung on the rack above the fireplace to be dry for morning. Many were the times I had to stay off school after an 'accident', because mom couldn't get my knickers dry. She had a horror of damp clothes and was so afraid of us 'catching our deaths of cold'. Any 'potatoes' (holes) in our socks must also be darned before morning.

Kneeling in our nighties in front of the fire, we submitted to further torture as our hair was combed with a fine toothcomb, heads bent and necks aching over a newspaper spread to catch head lice and nits. But it was fun to crack the lice and see the dots of blood on the newspaper. Endowed with thick, baby-fine-fly-away hair, toothcombing was torture almost beyond endurance, bringing tears of pain to the eyes to drop among the nits.

Nor was the torture over yet. Wax must be poked out of ears with the aid of the blunt end of a hair-grip. Scraped ear drums gave the same sensation as chalk scraped on a black-board, and made my teeth 'water'. Mom was anything but gentle, and it is miraculous that all five of us still possess excellent hearing forty years on.

All sweet and clean, shiny and scrubbed, we were lined up for 'dosing'. Each child, well or ill, must on Friday night swallow the following: One Aspro, One Little Lung Healer, One Teaspoonful of Milk of Magnesia, and One Teaspoonful of pure, unadulterated Cod Liver Oil. Yuk! Keith pretended to like the latter, smacking his little lips in anticipation. I, of course, gagged and squirmed, earning another slap.

'Look at Keith. 'E don't make no fuss. Yer'd think you was the Babby'.

Now came the good bit. Each child received a fat, single square of Cadbury's Dairy Milk Chocolate, to be nibbled sucked and savoured for a full five minutes. Sometimes it was a Mars Bar cut into six pieces. That treat lasted even longer as we relished the different layers.

A hot milky drink for all, and up the 'wooden hill', one of us carrying a crock chamber pot until the dreadful night when I tripped over my over-long nightie and fell, shatter-ing the pot to smithereens. What a good hiding I got for that piece of carelessness. Mom rarely spared the rod but she really went to town on me that time, raining blows all over my body and head, screaming and shouting in hysterical exhaustion. Even at the tender age of five or six I realised fully the enormity of my crime, knowing that that chamber pot could not be replaced. It was the enamel bucket from now on.

Tucked up in our beds and cots we sleepily said our 'Gentle Jesus' prayers, 'God Bless Mommy, God Bless Daddy, God bless everybody. Please make me a good girl (Oh, would He-ever!) For ever more Amen'. Then snug-gled down, top to toe with Keith in the big iron cot we shared until we scratched each other's faces with our toe nails. Left in the dreaded dark we whispered to each other, knowing better than to make a noise. If mom had to climb those stairs again in her exhausted state she would hit us all unmercifully. She was so tired. So very tired. It was a lesson in self-control, and collective punishment. It was no good calling mom if you wet the bed, as I did, nightly. You just lay in it until the morning, shifting your body about to try to find a dry spot. I would finally sleep on my hands and knees, bottom in the air, waking with agonising pins and needles and later inheriting a legacy of rheumaticky joints.

One bath-night stands out for all time. We three girls were in the bath, and dad was home on leave. He came into the bathroom with a big floor-scrubbing brush and laughingly set about 'washing' me. The harsh bristles tore into my tender skin as the 'game' turned into a nightmare. Mom rushed in to see what was happening, only to be told 'That mardy little bugger hasn't got any sense of humour'.

Was it that night, or another night, we three girls were left alone in the bath, laughing and playing, when suddenly I heard my mom screaming. I recall clambering over the high rim and running, naked and dripping, through the kitchen. I stopped suddenly, wide-eyed and terrified. Dad was towering over mom, who was lying on the floor in the living room doorway, arms raised to shield herself from his fists. I screamed and screamed for him to 'leave her alone please, leave her alone'. Margaret appeared and led me back into the bath, where I sucked the flannel to comfort myself and tried to push the dreadful images from my mind. I so wanted to make believe it hadn't happened. But at night, when I tried to sleep, the pictures kept coming back behind my closed eyelids.

At other times I would witness dad mauling my mother's breasts, or pulling her roughly onto his lap on the settee, attempting to put his hand up her skirt. On one of these occasions I heard him say something that I did not understand at the time, but would never forget. The words were, 'I've got a lucky charm. Do you want to charm it?'. I recognised the innuendo in dad's voice, saw the fear on my mother's face, and knew he was doing 'dirty things' that she didn't like. That time she struggled free, saying 'Stop it, Jack. The kids are 'ere. STOP IT'. Much later, I realised how she must have been torn between submitting to his excessive sexual demands, or refusing him and knowing he would get sex elsewhere. It was Hobson's choice, especially after experiencing V.D.

I must have been very little, perhaps only three, when I first 'knew' about sex. For some reason my cot was beside my parents' bed. Perhaps I was ill. I suddenly awakened in the darkness to whispered arguments and scuffling. I heard my father say 'I'll have to get you out of bed to do you, if you don't lie still'.

I heard mom sobbing quietly, and pleading for him 'not to waken the babby'. I instinctively knew I must not move or make a sound, and just lay there rigid with fear until I fell asleep, knowing my mom was being hurt and I could do nothing to help her.

How deep do these impressions go? What harm do they do? For myself, it is almost certain they helped to account for my own messy relationships with men. Nothing can ever wipe out the memories that come back, unbidden, haunting the adult long after the child has grown. Of course one wants to forget, but it is like wishing for the moon. Unthinking people say 'It's the past. Forget it'. If only one could. They don't understand; how could they? They haven't 'walked in my shoes'.

CHAPTER NINE

# Walks in the Black Country.

Catkins heralded the spring. Elongated, baby-soft, silver green droplets of condensed winter-weak sunlight. Now the weather was warmer I didn't mind the almost-daily walk with Big Sister, walks to get us from under mom's feet. Off we'd troop across the estate and out towards the railway. No houses here—just vast expanses of sewage, treated and untreated, giving off a pungent smell. But there were wild flowers and trees in abundance, unbelievably green and bursting with rude health. As we walked we passed many enterprising gardeners barrowing the aromatic stuff for their gardens and allotments.

Big Sister, weighed down with an unwieldy pram and a scruffy mongrel dog, busily kept us from running into the road or falling into the sewage, whilst simultaneously pacifying the baby by endlessly dipping his dummy into a cup of sugar. Keith rode at the bottom of the pram, matchstick legs too fragile even for his frail body. I hung onto the pram handle while sister Josy, a year my senior, wandered silently and dreamily ahead. She was an aloof, dour, secretive child, so different from my brash voluble self.

In the 'well' of the pram would be doorsteps of bread, each with a scrape of margarine and the merest hint of jam. To complete the feast, a couple of pop bottles containing water, but on red-letter days it could be well-watered-down Welfare Orange Juice.

We'd all help to haul the pram over the first railway footbridge, and if we were very lucky, when we got to the top a goods train would clatter beneath us, enveloping us in

38

clouds of steam. High up on the slatted wooden bridge I entered a rosy dream-world where harshness and ugliness had no place; my world transformed into something of mystery and strange beauty. And afterwards I was filled with an indefinable anguish deep within my being when reality made an unwelcome return.

Down on the other side of the bridge we went and off over the 'Nine Bridges' which spanned the flooded expanse of sewage. Later on in the spring we would gather tadpoles in jam-jars tied up with string. Sometimes rough boys would be at the 'Nine Bridges', busily engaged in throwing stones at mature frogs or blowing them up with straws of grass until they burst. Then blind rage would envelop me. The bright day would darken over and I would know what Hell was like. Helpless frogs were being tortured by mindless, obscene giants, and I was crucified by their silent agony. God didn't exist-there was NO ONE to save these innocent helpless creatures-yet still I screamed my supplications frantically begging and pleading. But God didn't listen.

There was a narrow river that we passed on the way home, overhung by a huge Oak tree with a stout rope attached to its lower branch. We called it 'The Trapeze'-taking it in turns to sit on the big knot at the end of the rope, to swing giddily out over the water and the far bank. Brave boys leaped off at this point but I had not the courage-and I hated myself for my cowardice. I was a tom-boy, everybody said so. But I knew I had not the necessary skill and fearlessness. Or perhaps my defective sight obscured the safe landing place?

Some weekends Margaret traipsed with us across the Common. It was a long walk: about a mile to get right off the estate in the opposite direction from the Sewage Farm. Sometimes Fat Aunt took us if she was 'on the box' or on holiday from the buses. I didn't like her much. She was handsome in her clippie uniform, inevitable Woodbine clamped between carmine lips. She had the voice of a Drill Sergeant. Laden with containers for gathering whatever berries were in season we'd trek across the fields, deftly avoiding the cow-pats, until we came within sight of the canal. At the last stile we helped with the pram or pushchair, and then we were free.

The last two fields before the canal I called 'our' fields, the first a cornfield to be crossed blindly, straight as the crow flies, when the corn was at its full height. Oh, another world of smells-sticky rasping ears of Corn and Barley dragging at hair and teasing along cheeks. But my very favourite was the 'last' field. In the Buttercup season it was an enchanted place. Millions and millions of glistening butter-yellow dishes adoring the sun, to be picked and chucked under each others chins chanting 'Do you like butter' and if you did the glistening yellow leaves reflected on your skin. I hated treading their perfect faces but it was unavoidable as I raced away from the others – to prance and shout with sheer delight at the heady joy of being alive amidst such sunlit beauty. Exhausted I would lie flat, Buttercups forming a fence around my body-snuggling me, shrouding me, while above stretched the sky, forever-away. 'Please God, let me stay here forever. I never want to go back, never'. But Fat Aunt was calling from the canal bank, 'Come on Joanny, stop yer bloody dawdling'.

One glorious, memorable day, Fat Aunt slipped down the steep bank at the side of the canal towpath, overbalancing as she reached for the fattest, juiciest berries, her tree-trunk legs thrusting clean through a huge patch of nettles and thorns. She screamed for us to haul her out but we just fell about the towpath, howling with mirth; sick with barely suppressed laughter. 'Serve yer right yer fat bugger' whispered little innocent-looking Keith between gasps. Five fat, red, finger marks across his scraggy bare legs soon bore silent testimony to his personal ill-will.

We watched the barges being towed through the water by the huge, patient horses, muffled heavy footsteps clip-clopping on the impacted earth mingling with the shouts of bargees and their brown-skinned children. The ripples of shock-waves disturbed the canal banks, causing the reeds to dance and glide, weaving strange patterns under the green, mysterious water. The drone of bees among the wild flowers, the whisper of leaves stroking each other to a tender, whispered tune, -all was bliss. These were sounds of summer in the Black Country, a mile or so from the concrete jungle that housed our home, our personal war-zone. A place where I would still rather be, for solace, than anywhere else on earth.

Then, as the sun went down, the long, tiring haul back home. Over the stile crawl five children, sunburned and sleep-laden; each holding locked inside themselves their own personal memory of such a day, to be taken out from the secret places of the soul and gloated over, or grieved for, in the agony of years to come.

CHAPTER TEN

# The Old Garden.

The garden was our main playground in the early years. Our house was on a corner site and consequently the garden was bigger than others in the council block. It was completely surrounded by a crenellated cement-grey breeze-block wall about four feet high, and it was a secretive magic world that we children inhabited. Here we lived out our infant fantasies, individually and together, and sowed enchanted seeds in memory to be garnered in the dark years ahead.

The weeds grew unchecked. Masses of soaring purple Willow Herb and Fairy Fingers stabbed the sky, Cow-Parsley and high whispering grass arched above us. Sun-bright Dandelions and delicate Daisies, yellow-eyed and pink-edged, starred the flattened places that were our dens. Yellow Tansy and Dog-Daisies stood stiffly like still-life studies, tempting the eye, while bright blue Periwinkles wove a tattered carpet for our feet.

We each had our own separate den, linked together by busily-trodden pathways. Margaret had taught us certain courtesies to be observed when visiting one another, which Keith and I regularly flaunted.

Recalling my own patch of earth, I feel again the tug of ears of grass on bare skin, see the awesome intricate beauty of cuckoo-spit and spiders' webs. Picking up a thick blade of grass to whistle through, the razor edge cut deeply and painlessly into my finger, bright-red blood mingling with the dark green. The tall Nettles had dusty, hairy leaves and the white/purple flowers, when sucked, tasted like sugar-water. I had never tasted honey. When I did so, many years later, I immediately identified it as 'nettle-nectar'. White lumps speckled arms and legs, surrounded by a pale green area where Dock leaves had been rubbed to ease the nettle-sting.

My den boasted a collection of broken glass and pottery, carefully set out for maximum effect on rusty tin lids. Washed with spit and rubbed on my frock, they gave off brilliant rays of light and colour. Beside the lids stood a jam jar containing freshly picked Dandelions. We had been told that the milk from the Dandelion stems made you wet the bed if you got it on your fingers. I wet the bed anyway, so felt it didn't much matter.

Here, in this my secret world, I wove intricate cages out of grass to house my collection of butterflies, newly caught each day. I was careful not to rub the white dust off their wings as Margaret had told me this would stop them from flying. In my imagination my cages were beautiful mansions that my butterflies were happy to inhabit. I sang and talked to my prettily-winged 'friends' for hours, before freeing them at the end of the game, glorying in their delicate fragile beauty. They were mine and I loved them so. It was half a life-time before I fully understood that love stands for freedom, not imprisonment.

Dog often wandered into my den, to stay and snooze awhile and dream her doggy dreams. The cat would almost certainly be with me, often under duress, below a cardboard box weighted with stones. As I go back in time I can hear again the drone of bumble-bees and blue-bottles, the rub of grass on grass, the rattle of seed-pods. Lying flat on my tummy I could watch, with a sort of clinical detachment, the scurrying ear-wigs, beetles and ants. Or, rolled over, I would contemplate the heavens, so vast after that other Lilliputian insect world. From what direction would Jesus come I wondered? For our Sunday School had drummed into us that come He most certainly would, one day or another. I hoped and prayed very much that it would not be today. Today was good . . .

Sometimes I crept along the passage that connected my den with Margaret's, in order to eavesdrop on my sisters. She and Josy often played together in Margaret's den, dramatic games that I could only share as a secret on-looker. One day I particularly recall: Josy was wearing a red pixie hat over her golden curls, the long ties of which hung loosely down her back and were weighted at the ends with scraps of ribbon. These, I gathered, were her 'pig-tails', to be nonchantly tossed over her shoulders in a haughty manner. In this game she was a lady called Guinevere and Margaret a man called Arthur. I knew he must be a king because he had a cake-tin on his head, and wore a cloak (an old curtain) round his shoulders. Arthur was very stern, standing with arms folded, while Guinevere knelt at his feet, begging for forgiveness, tears streaming down her face. Carried away by the desperate sobbing I rushed forward, begging Arthur to forgive the poor lady.

Banished as usual from their 'Court' I wandered along to Josy's den. I knew from past experience what I would find there, and felt sick and cold as I entered the flattened patch. Half-end-duckers (broken house bricks) were neatly set out into squares of differing sizes. These were Josy's Hospital wards, housing green cabbage caterpillars and brown earth-worms she would have collected fresh that morning. I shivered at the sliver of broken glass Josy kept for cutting them in half before placing them in the wards 'to get better'. A jam jar stood forgotten beside the 'wards' and inside were the corpses of about fifty earth-worms that had fried in the hot sun.

Suddenly I hurt all over with anger, pity and frustration, I hated Josy−HATED her. I wanted to cut her up so she would know what it felt like. A few days later she would beat me physically for releasing a jar-full of newly-collected worms. Margaret, hearing the fight, patiently explained that I, too, was cruel for caging butterflies. I never kept them again, and was haunted by visions of their desperately-fluttering wings for a long time. I wanted to make it up to them but I didn't know how. I still don't.

Next I visited Keith's den beside the palings separating our garden from my godmother's house. Her youngest son, Bobby, was the same age as our Keith, and he and my brother were playing cars. They had built a ramp of house-bricks on either side of the fence and Bobby's collection of

Dinky cars zoomed and crashed, to the happy sound of the boys' car noises, '. . . Brrrrmmmmmm. Berrrummmmmmm'. 'Beruooooommmm'. Tall Golden Rod growing on the other side of the palings arched way up in the sky, and I almost over-balanced in an effort to stroke their dusty flowers. Mom called from the back door a few yards away. She stood with the Babby on one arm and four door-steps in her other hand, to be distributed by me around the dens.

How bright are the colours of early remembered childhood. How white the bread, how red the jam. The grass would never be so green again, nor the sky so blue. The world that day was sweet and fresh and sparkling, remembered images etched around as if in charcoal, filled in with colours fresh from the Artist's Palette.

Trudging up the path at the side of the house on my way to give out the sandwiches, I took great care not to tread on the cracks in between the paving slabs. If I did I must cross my fingers and wish hard that I wouldn't die. And of course I wouldn't. Ever.

In 1947 the Council threatened tenants with eviction unless they cultivated their gardens. Father mustered his troops and ordered them to dig and hoe, to plant and sow. It was like digging our own graves and in a way perhaps it was so.

Thirty years later I returned to Shelley Road and asked the present occupants for permission to look around their garden, explaining that I had been born in that house. It didn't take me long to walk around; it was so very small. Willow Herb again flourished unchecked beside the gate, reminding me of its common name of Bomb Blossom. It was noted for its ability to thrive on bomb sites, its purple beauty soon miraculously transforming the ugly scars. It symbolised, for me, survival during my own protracted postwar period of reconstruction.

## CHAPTER ELEVEN

# Lost Innocence.

It was a lovely sunny day, a Sunday, when my education in life began in earnest. I was about seven years old and had just returned from Sunday School with my brother and sisters. Dad always had a lie-down on Sunday afternoons, after returning from the pub, and it seemed mom joined him because the door was always locked when we got home. When mom finally opened it she was dishevelled and edgy.

On this particular Sunday, as mom opened the back door, dad could be heard shouting from the bedroom to 'Send the buggers out into the garden'. Knowing mom always obeyed dad, off we dutifully trooped. A few minutes later I fell whilst jumping off the wall, cutting my knee quite badly on the rusty cog of a bicycle lying hidden in the grass.

Mom, ears ever alert to one of her children blarting, soon appeared and led me into the house to bathe my knee. As she bandaged the wound in her rough and ready fashion I heard dad's voice rumbling from upstairs, through the open hall door-way.

'Send her up here, I'll see to her'.

Oh, joy. My dad wanted to comfort me! I'd always known it would happen one day. Up I jumped, knee forgotten, and was already up the first three stairs before mom caught me and hauled me back into the living room, slamming the hall door behind her. It all happened so quickly I was dumb-struck. 'Me dad wants to love me better . . . it ain't fair'.

Through my tears of self-pity I suddenly became aware of the look on mom's face as she stood there with her back to the stairs' door, barring my way. Finally she pulled herself together and was able to spell out to me the dreadful warning she must give to all her daughters, if we were to escape her own awful fate.

As I listened the lovely day darkened and the room grew chill. I left that room, minutes later, infinitely older and wiser than when I had entered it. Dragging leaden feet up the garden and into my den, hidden in the long grass I began to sort out the jumble of words drumming in my ears. I wished I could wipe my mind clean of mom's warning and confession, yet I dimly realised that this would never be possible. Forty years later it still stands out in inverted commas in my mind.

'Joanny' mom had begged. 'Listen to me. It's very important. Never, never goo to yer dad's bed or let 'im touch ya . . . stay safe. Stay away from 'im . . . 'e might 'urt ya like me dad did me. LISTEN . . . When I wuz a little gairl, not much older'n you, me dad started to . . . interfere with me, when me mom wuz out. 'E told me not to tell nobody or 'e'd kill me . . .'.

We had a word for penis, it was 'peter' and I knew both my brothers had one. Inexorably, tears streaming down her face, mother continued.

'Me dad pushed 'is peter inside me tummy . . . 'e layd on top of me . . . 'e did it every time 'e got me on me own. Me mom wuz out a lot cleaning, and the other kids wuz only babbies. . . . When I wuz ten I got scarlit fever and nearly died. When I wuz in 'ospital some doctor noticed a swelling at the top of me leg . . . asked me mom about it. Me dad never done it again'.

What had this got to do with me?, with my dad? I must have asked.

'Yer dad knows what me dad done to me, and 'e says 'e'll do it to you gairls if I don't do everything 'e says . . . I've give 'im the rent money . . . 'e's just never satisfied. Promise me,' she whispered, 'Promise me ya'll never . . . I don't want it to 'appen to you.'

Now I, too, had been sentenced for life, with no chance of reprieve for good behaviour. Guilt and disgust would, intermittently, be my most constant companions for decades to come. I was tainted twice over, through two generations. Later I would learn of a third generation. I wondered if it was hereditary. What a legacy to pass on to future generations!

I recall walking round the corner of Shelley Road to my special rose bush and inhaling deeply its sweet clean smell, then returning to the garden and seeking out Margaret. Seeing my distress, my big sister roughly tried to find words of comfort, after I had gabbled out my story. Her ten year old face was tired and wise and old. She brushed her hand over her forehead as mom did in times of stress.

'It was time yer knew, our Jo. It's safer that way. Now, when me dad calls ya to cum to 'is bed or anything, yer'll 'ave to act like ya aint 'eard, like me and Josy do. Now off ya goo an' play'.

She returned to her den in the garden, immediately resuming the fantasy game she was playing with Josy. From their posh accents I knew they were playing a game they called 'Patricia and Florence'. In this game they were wealthy ladies, like the ones we saw at the local Greenpark Church, all big hats and cut-glass accents. They wouldn't let me into this game, either. Said I was too young. But even then I knew that fantasy was not a door through which I could escape.

The following Sunday morning mom was busy making breakfast and scuttling about in the 'back kitchen'. Lying in bed, half dozing, I dimly heard dad's voice calling from his bedroom, His tones were purring and gentle.

'Come here Joanny. Come and have a bit of love from your daddy before you get up'.

Dozily I went through to him and cuddled up under the blankets, hungry as always for loving physical contact, for loving arms around me. In my half-asleep state I had forgotten mom's warning. I suppose I didn't want to believe it anyway, subconsciously. Slowly dad shifted me on top of his body to 'make me more comfortable' and began moving himself rythmically against my weight. His breathing became loud and gasping and suddenly I was wide awake.

'Dad. Don't'. I pleaded.

'Shush, shush'. he soothed, his voice like velvet, 'Don't

let your mommy hear you'.

With strength borne of hate, betrayal, and sheer anger at my own stupidity, I struggled free. I raced to the doorway, then turned. From far away I heard my voice saying 'You'm a dirty man, aint ya dad'? I knew I shouldn't have said it but I couldn't stop myself. Truth would always cause me more trouble than lies. His answering bellow shocked and propelled me hell-for-leather downstairs.

'Get out, you cross-eyed little bugger. Get out'.

Sitting in my garden den, mulling over the events of the last few minutes, I began to piece together a sort of jig-saw in my mind. This incident had not been the first time dad had tried to interfere with me. Funny how I had pushed it out of my mind until now.

A few months previously dad had volunteered to take me to his work, one Saturday morning. At that time he worked within cycling distance of Shelley Road, over behind the railway, where he was Factory Manager. Mom had will-ingly let me go thinking, I suppose, that I was too young to be at risk. Sitting on the cross-bar of his bicycle, whizzing along by the 'Nine Bridges', I was in a sort of seventh heaven. Dad had never taken me out before although he regularly took Margaret and Josy to 'The Bull's Head' where he drank on Sundays. Now I knew his neglect of me wasn't because I was cross-eyed but because I had been too little. I can still recall my feelings of intense joy during that ride. I had always known he would be a Real Daddy one day.

When we arrived at his work he introduced me to the staff. I felt very important indeed, and was careful to be on my best behaviour and not show myself up as I usually did. Dad took me to the Canteen and got me an ice-cream from the fridge, then led me into his office and patted his knee, all smiles and softness. Happily I obeyed, cuddling deep into his jacket and savouring my ice-cream. I still don't recall what my dad did after that that so bothered me, but I do recall the sudden knowledge that I didn't like it one bit and no longer wanted to sit on his lap. Somehow I got to the door and tried to open it. It was locked. I was sobbing now and dad said I was 'just a mardy little bugger, that's why nobody ever takes you anywhere'. He said he'd never take me to work again but I didn't care.

Rummaging about in my mind, digging up bits I'd tried to bury, a murky picture of my dad began to emerge. Still, it was hard to accept that he would never love me like a real dad, that he only wanted my body. I felt old.

He never really assaulted me again, although he did maul us girls about occasionally on the excuse of 'tickling' us. We soon learned to avoid him. We grew wise to the 'Feel in my pocket for my handkie my hands are dirty' ploy. There would, we knew, be no bottom to the pocket, just a hard sweaty piece of male flesh. Sometimes, in the early years, he indulged in rare horse-play with us, playing 'hide and seek' around the house. On catching us girls his podgy hands would feel sweatily around flat bosoms. We soon learned to avoid him altogether, much to mom's relief.

If only such men would realise that, long after their urgent bodily pleasures have become a limp memory, assaulted children will continue to feel tainted and abnormal, possibly for the rest of their lives. There is, for me, no crime worse than incest. It destroys so utterly the very core of the assaulted human being. It betrays a sacred trust. It harms the child forever.

My father is a sick old man and my grandfather dead. Neither will damage another child but the repercussions of their selfish acts continue to hurt my mother, her daughters, their partners and children. Even if we don't share our dread secret our children are still harmed in subtle ways. And by keeping our secret locked inside, we burden ourselves with a guilt that is not, and never was, ours.

Unthinking people say 'Forget the past. It is dead'. If only it were. Each time I read of, or hear of, children being sexually molested, feelings of not just anger assail me. Triggered memories, sense of betrayal, lost innocence, are all jumbled up, the crime made more evil by the knowledge that that child is scarred for life, mentally and emotionally if not physically. Even today people still do not communicate truly with each other when it comes to incest. I have always talked openly about my own experience, finding it very therapeutic in the early years. Yet I have rarely heard anyone admit to a personal knowledge of the subject. Knowing the horrifying statistics in this matter, I know now I am not 'unusual' or a 'freak', yet were it not for the published figures I would most certainly have continued to believe that I was.

For the record, both my father and grandfather were of above average intelligence. Both were well read and had travelled away from their narrow roots. It was not ignorance, then, that led to their crimes, but sheer animal lust. One avant-garde psychiatrist tried to tell me, when I was twenty and first sought help, that incest was 'just an excess of fatherly affection'. 'Balls' I retorted in a rare moment of coarseness. That expletive was, I still feel, far nearer to the truth than her trite Freudian explanation.

These experiences in my early life, and my mother's, had a devastating 'knock-on' effect. My mother never recovered, spending most of her later life on drugs and in and out of mental hospitals. And so I lost her. There could be no loving relationship with my father or grandfather. Also, it is possible that my father's guilt later caused him to alienate himself from the rest of his brothers and sisters. Therefore our family grew up in isolation, although surrounded by extended family. The loneliness for me lasted half a lifetime. I was lucky.

Just recently, listening to a programme about atrocities committed in Concentration Camps, particularly experiments on children, I tried to get incest into perspective. To see it as just one of many crimes. I couldn't. Incest stands alone. The torturers of the children in the Nazi Camps were not *personally known* to the child. In crimes of incest the very foundation and core of such children is violated, their trust totally betrayed, their future relationships warped.

CHAPTER TWELVE

# Going to the Pictures.

After the War had ended Margaret began taking us three older children to the pictures on Saturday afternoons. These outings became the high spot of the week for years to come.

Soon after lunch Margaret gathered together her charges and set off with us in crocodile formation, down Shelley Road and along past the Big School. It was best to avert one's eyes from the huge open water tank for use if Incendiary Bombs landed, as it was frequently utilised to dispose of unwanted cats and dogs.

Like the Pied Piper Margaret led us on up Brookspill Road, a busy main road linking Walsall with Birmingham, still in those days edged on one side by a glorious field of Cowslips, Buttercups and Bog-Irises, the meandering brook alive with newts and darting fish. Over the traffic lights we marched, Margaret holding fast the smaller children's hands.

'Bet it's 'Old Muvver Riley'' hazarded Keith.

'Bet ya 'taint. Bet ya it's 'Lassie Cum 'ome ', I retorted hopefully. Keith would have none of this.

'I know warr it'll be. It'll be Roy Rogers an' Trigger. Bang. Bang. You'm dead, Joanny . . .'

He pulled his hand free from Margaret's restraining grasp and began shooting from an imaginary Colt at his hip. I started to do an Indian War Dance, whooping and waving an invisible tomahawk . . .

'Pack it in, you two. Cum 'ere, you'll get run over- then we'll never get to the pikchers. JOAN. KEITH . . .

I shan't take you two to the pikchers again if you can't be'ave. I won't tell you again'.

52

'They're just little animals' murmured Josy, looking up from the book she always carried when we went out. A precocious child, she was reading Enid Blyton's 'Mallory Towers' books and spoke in the manner of Boarding School girls.

'Personally, Margaret, I don't know why you bother with them'.

At the top of the hill, just past the school, one of the terraced houses had been turned into a tuck shop. Margaret doled out a precious half-penny each and in we dashed. On tip-toes at the counter we stood, goggle-eyed and spoiled for choice. For a half-penny we could purchase two wooden sticks or one shiny black 'shoe-lace' of liquorice. A yellow, sweet powder called 'Kkali' could be had in a twist of paper, into which would be dipped a moistened finger. There were Sherbert Dabs and Bull's-Eyes, Gob-Stoppers, white Sugar Mice or grinning 'False Teeth' sweets and sweet Cigarettes.

Margaret was busily surveying the great glass sweet jars with a practised eye, her hand clutching the coupon books without which no confectionery could be purchased. 'I'll take a quarter o' Dolly Mixtures, please'.

'Oh, Margaret. We 'ad them last wik. Dain't we, Keith? Let's 'ave sum Pear Drops- they last ever so much lunger. Please Margaret . . .'

'Be quiet, Jo. You can't 'ave Pear Drops. You swallowed one 'olesale last week. You dain't 'alf gie me a fright. Lucky that man was there to 'old you upside down. No, Dolly Mixtures are safer for you little 'uns'.

The Shopman, Mr Beard, scooped out a handful of sweets, weighing them carefully on his balance-scales and pouring the sweets into a white paper cone.

'Cum on, yow kids. Oy aint gorr all day. What yow 'aving?'.

A life-time spent dishing out pennorths of sweets to generations of choosy children had left Mr Beard with an almost pathological hatred of youngsters. He clicked his false teeth impatiently.

'I'll 'ave an 'alf-penny bottle o' pop, please' I told Mr Beard, eyes averted slightly from his face. I tried hard not to look at the sandy hairs poking out of his nostrils, and most especially I tried not to look at the unsightly goitre that bulged above his starched collar. I rarely succeeded.

Mr Beard selected a small empty bottle from the shelf behind him and filled it with carbonated flavoured coloured water into which he inserted a straw.

'Now mind and gi' me the bottle back in a minute or Oy'll 'ave yer guts for garters . . .' Bubbles danced up, tickling my nose as I gulped greedily at the salty sharp liquid.

"Urry up, Jo. We'll be late. . . .'

Another half-mile along the road and we were there. The Plaza was situated at Stafford Green, half-way to Walsall. An ugly, dirty white building set in the centre of a row of grubby shops like a single discoloured front molar in a mouthful of decaying teeth.

Even though we got to the cinema before the doors opened there was always a queue of urchins stretching right around the Green, a tiny strip of grass boasting an underground toilet. Margaret shepherded us neatly into line, forbidding us to join the other children in their 'common' cat-calls and jeers.

"Ello, Keith Stafford. 'As yer big sister changed yer nappie?'. 'Keith, Keith, rabbit teeth'. Keith was always the butt of bully boys at school and they plagued him mercilessly.

'Tek no notice our Keith. They ain't werth it'. I attempted to impose myself between tiny Keith and the bully boys, while Margaret whispered a reprimand to him for wiping his nose and eyes on his sleeve. My heart went out to my brother, standing beside me with shiny fair head bowed, shoulders hunched over his concave chest. None of us had possessed a top-coat since late infancy, and Keith always looked pinched and cold. He had a habit, when nervous, of holding the muscle of his left upper arm with his right hand. Under the thin jacket I knew there was a permanently sore purple bruise where dad always 'playfully' punched him in passing. It would, over the years, deepen in colour and mark him for life.

'Cheer up our Keith. It's Tarzan wots on. An' 'Old Muvver Riley''. Keith's tiny features lit up as I imparted this information, gleaned from the display of lurid stills pinned up in a glass case just outside the foyer. We had shuffled nearer and Margaret was counting out the eight pennies, all that was left of the whole precious shilling of our joint pocket money. The shabbily liveried doorman strode importantly along the queue.

'Any more for the tuppennies? Cum on, Oy ain't gorr all day'. Margaret exchanged her pennies for tickets at the kiosk and ushered us ahead of her into the darkened cinema. A crone of an usherette, 'Passing Cloud' dangling from slack bottom lip, snatched the tickets and pointed the beam of her torch wordlessly to four vacant up-tipped seats on the back row.

'Blow it, Margaret. I'll never be able to see prop'ly . . .' I whined.

'Stop grizzling our Jo. I can't 'elp it. Sit down and shurrup. You shouldn't have dawdled so much at the shop. You won't be told'. Margaret reached over and cupped my nose with the clean rag she always carried for her charges.

'Blow your nose. Shhhhh. the pikcher's started'.

Narrowing my eyes into slits and tilting back my head I discovered I could see quite well, if uncomfortably. The Fire Curtain was already raised and the sound of drum-beats loudly filled the air. The whirr of the projector could be heard above the sound track. My eyes followed the beam of light from the screen to high up above the balcony, reflecting particles of dust and gobs of spit aimed at us from the posher kids lording it over us in the Gods. One day I vowed, when I'm rich, I'll take us swanking into the threepennies.

Soon the flickering image on the screen held us in thrall, the black and white larger than life Tarzan and Jane peopling our own imaginary world. Open-mouthed we breathlessly joined Tarzan as he managed, in the nick of time, to grab a handy vine and soar safely above the herd of stampeding rogue elephants.

There would be a loud exhalation of breath from the audience as Tarzan landed deftly on his tree-house platform. We felt as sick as Jane looked as she knelt to examine the tusk-wound oozing gallons of black blood all over the bamboo platform, and now spilling over her manicured hands as she attempted to staunch the flow. 'Jane help Tarzan. Jane make better . . .' Out over the jungle she swung, her long hair swinging prettily behind her. How I envied her her long hair, American accent, effortless grace and Tarzan's affections.

As Tarzan and Jane took on leopards and tigers, prised open the jaws of man-eating crocodiles or grappled with gigantic snakes, we children fought with them every inch of the way. At the end of the film I felt exhausted and elated. Tarzan and Jane had miraculously survived, unscathed, to love and fight another day. What a relief! We would see them again next Saturday.

There was only a short interval between films as few children could afford the ice-creams carried on a tray around the neck of the usherette. Margaret carefully shared out the Dolly Mixtures and these small sweets were savoured and sucked slowly, releasing a delicate scent like violets or roses.

Next 'Old Mother Riley' filled the screen, all wrinkled stockings, wispy white hair in a bun and tiny black hat firmly secured under her chin. Her darling daughter Kitty was the innocent foil for Mother's zany antics, sly drollery and whimsical wheedlings. We rocked in our seats with mirth, breathless and exhausted by the end of the film.

On other Saturdays there would be 'The Adventures of Batman'. The cloaked, tight-hosed figure of Batman, slit-eyed behind his inevitable mask, zoomed effortlessly in and out of sky-scraper windows perilously high above the New York traffic, aided and abetted by the trusty Robin. The frequent falls of Keith and I off the shed roof owed much to their influence, our old-curtain cloaks never billowing and bearing us gently to the ground as Batman's did.

Shirley Temple didn't impress me much, reminding me as she did of sister Josy, all prissy curls, neat clothes and coy dimples. I didn't care for her goody-goody deeds or her sickly-sweet, baby-voiced singing. I did however, envy her her soft toys, wishing I had a teddy to tuck under MY arm for comfort.

I dreaded the 'Lassie Come Home' films, reducing me as they always did to blind anger and murderous rage when he was frightened or hurt by the 'baddies'. During one scene, where Lassie was kidnapped, Margaret had much difficulty in restraining me from rushing down to the screen to rescue him.

'It's only a film, Jo . . . don't be soft . . .' Margaret didn't understand. Nobody did.

At the end of the film there were always copious tears of relief as the faithful Lassie snuggled safely into his owner's arms. I hated crying in front of people, suffering agonised embarrassment until the tears were willed away.

Keith and I loved the Westerns, especially Roy Rogers and his trusty steed Trigger. These films were all blood and thunder, dastardly deeds committed by impassive Indian Braves, flying tomahawks and circles of covered wagons eternally pierced by flying arrows. The women in these films seemed soppy and cowardly, hiding behind their men or wagons, faint-hearted and feminine. Not me, I was out there alongside the men, squinting down the barrel of my shotgun and mowing down Indians like corn at harvest-time all oily hands, mud-streaked face and wind-blown hair.

All too soon the matinée ended and we joined the jostling crowd heading for the bright cold light of day out on the Green . . . and back to harsh reality. The mean streets seemed even more ugly and Shelley Road unbearable.

'It's not fair . . . not fair . . . Not Fair . . .' my mind hammered out the phrase in time to my leaden footsteps as I trailed reluctantly behind my sisters and brother.

'Cum on, Jo. Stop your dreamin'. You just missed that lamp-post. Pick up your feet, you'm slothering your shoes again. Mom aint got no money for mendin' 'em'.

Down the long steep hill we trooped, back over the traffic lights and past the brook. Four shabby children locked inside their separate worlds. Josy, nose inches from the inevitable book, deftly side-stepping lamp-posts; Margaret, mind occupied with the practicalities of keeping us children safe and planning the shopping budget for the week; Keith, held fast by Margaret's restraining hand, walking along with a strange jogging gait–and I knew if he hadn't messed his trousers again he was riding Trigger.

I tagged reluctantly behind, feeling isolated and miserable, automatically avoiding the 'unlucky' cracks in the pavement, simultaneously hurrying my steps in order to pass the next lamp-post before the approaching lorry. The post must be touched before the lorry passed or I'd . . . I'd . . . die.

'An ambulance, Joanny. Quick, 'ide yer nails' called Keith over his shoulder.

Dutifully I pressed my finger-tips into the palms of my hands, knowing I'd certainly die that instant if I didn't. Danger and death threatened constantly as we approached Shelley Road's concrete jungle. Tarzan's jungle of marauding lions and tigers I could cope with, given half a chance. Shelley Road was not to be borne.

Still, never mind. There was always next Saturday . . . I'd somehow survive until then.

CHAPTER THIRTEEN

# Children's Games.

The first remembered games of childhood, for most people, are the simple baby-games such as 'Pat-a-cake', 'Peep Bo', and 'Catch-a-ball'. Such games must have been played with young children since the dawn of creation, and will continue to be played so for eons to come. Unless, of course, some scientist can totally alter the innocent, simple, laughing, stumbling, tear-stained world of infancy.

Even our house in Shelley Road once rang with merry laughter during the dark days of the war, as mother and neighbours danced each succeeding baby upon their knees. 'Down, down, the deep blue sea. Catching fishes one . . . two . . . threeeeee' they chanted, and we dared to allow ourselves to be dangled upside-down, star fish hands securely held, quite safe in the knowledge that, on the count of three, we would be safely restored right-way-up. 'Again . . . Again . . .' the infant learned early to shout, to be humorously obeyed until the adult tired. The child never did.

In the garden, as soon as we could toddle, we learned to play with each other or amuse ourselves. We played marbles, with round stones, on the concrete slabbed path beside the house, or hop-scotch, drawing the numbers in with chalky stones. We also amused ourselves individually by bouncing an old tennis ball off the outside wall of the house, or swinging on a piece of rope tied to an overhead beam above the back-gate.

Keith and I regularly disobeyed mother by climbing onto the roof of the rickety garden shed, and just as regularly falling off. Hearing the thud of body on hard earth mom would rush out of the house, pick us up and inspect us for broken bones or other damage. Then she would give us a thorough good hiding.

'That'll teach ya to frighten the life out of me, ya little buggers'.

All of us children spent hours competing with each other in a complicated game we had evolved which involved jumping off the crenellated garden wall. We were rarely bored.

In the school playground we learned games played by generations of children before us. A favourite game at our Infant School required one bigger child to lean against the school wall, forming a human arch. We little children lined up in a crocodile and threaded our way beneath the 'arch' chanting:

"The big ship sails on the Illy Ally O.
The Illy Ally O. The Illy Ally O.
The big ship sails on the Illy Ally O
On the last day of September".

For 'Oranges and Lemons' we skipped through an arch made by two children, clasping their hands high above their heads:

"'Oranges and Lemons',
Said the Bells of St. Clemen's.
'I owe ya five farthin's',
Said the bells of St. Martin's . . ."

'Ring a Ring a Roses' was another favourite . . .

'Atishoo, atishoo, we all fall down' we trilled merrily, sublimely unaware of the song's dread origins, finally collapsing gleefully onto the dusty playground.

'What time is it Mr Wolf? What time is it Mr Wolf? . . .' we questioned in unison of our leader, marching ahead of us holding aloft a Dandelion that had gone to seed. 'ONE o'clock . . .' puffed our leader, 'TWO o'clock . . .', blowing hard on the dandelion-head until all the cotton-woolly glistening seeds were scattered. The leader then gave chase and caught one of us who then became leader.

How we enjoyed the giddy, breathless delights of 'Hide and Seek' and 'Tick', seeking and chasing each other in and out of the smelly school toilets.

There were definite seasons for street games. Who decreed the beginning or end of such 'seasons' goodness alone knew. It just happened, as swallows return or geese migrate. All of a sudden there would be a craze for 'Tops and Whips', the tops spinning giddily across the pavement, jumping over cracks and usually coming to grief in the gutter. Posher children sported shop-bought tops and whips, while we poorer children made do with tops that had seen service as Tizer bottle stoppers, made of pot and deeply threaded to accomodate the thong of the whip. We chalked circles of different colours on the tops, to delight the eye when the top was spun. Whips consisted of stout twigs and thin string.

As suddenly as this 'season' began it ended and 'Skipping' was all the rage, pavements and playgrounds ringing with the rhythmic sound of heavily-shod childish feet bouncing off unyielding concrete. Better-off children had skipping ropes adorned with wooden handles and tinkling bells, while we begged meagre lengths of clothes-line from our harassed mothers.

The best skipping games were played in the middle of the 'horse road'. In the early days the only traffic was horse-drawn and later, for many years, motor traffic was infrequent in Shelley Road. Two larger children or young adults stood opposite each other turning the yards of heavy rope in unison, while we children skipped in and out chanting:

"All in together, gairls,
This fine weather, gairls.
When we shout yer berthday,
Please fall out.
January . . . February . . .
March . . . April . . ."

Meaningless jingles were interspersed with traditional rhymes. What, I wonder, was the origin of:

"I like coffee, I like tea.
I like sitting on a black mon's knee.
Then the black mon said ta me
'Salt, Mustard. Vinegar. Pepper.
Salt, Mustard. Vinegar. Pepper.'"

The rope was turned faster and faster until the last skipper dropped out exhausted. When the two rope turners grew tired others took their place and the game lasted for hours.

As I write, I recall the distant sounds of happy laughter and skipping feet. So many impressions surface as I look back down the corridor of years to those early post-war days. Little girls modestly holding down the hems of dresses as they skipped to and fro, up and down, or clung to hair-ribbons that threatened to fall. The sound of the sharp slap of hemp upon shins, the whirr of the rope, the whack as it hit the tarmacadam. Children resting on the pavement to relieve the stitch in their sides before once more joining the fray. There was the feeling of achievement as one ran into the rope and began to skip, and anger and disappointment when clumsy feet fouled the rope.

'Film Stars' was played from one pavement to the opposite wall. The leader leaned on the wall and shouted out the initials of a famous film star. The first child to shout out the full name could take one pace forward. The first child to touch the leader was then 'in' for the next game.

We knew the names of most of the currently famous film stars from Cigarette Cards and Film Annuals that were swopped amongst the children. Film Stars' faces were almost as familiar to us as our own. Tyrone Power, Victor Mature, Cary Grant, James Mason, Alan Ladd, James Stewart and Stewart Granger were amongst my favourites. Betty Grable, Lana Turner, Rita Heyworth, Vera Ellen, Rosalind Russell, Deanna Durbin . . . all so young and glamorous. Like ourselves they would never grow old; they were immortal.

Swapping cigarette cards amongst ourselves and our friends involved a great deal of soul-searching and noisy haggling.

'Give us Stewart Graynja', Joanny. Yow can 'ave Bing Crosby for 'im. Yow ain't got 'im, 'ave ya?'

'No, shan't. Stewart Graynja's me favourite. I'll swap ya . . .'

'Cum on, our Jo, yer've already got four of 'im. Yow don't need all them. I'll let yar 'ave me best Alexis Smiff for Stewart Graynja'.'

'Gerroff. 'er's nobody. Alexis Smith ain't a big star like

Vera Ellen . . .'

With our cards spread out upon the pavement before us, we bribed and wheeled and dealed to make up complete sets. The faces of the film stars were all coloured an improbable pink, with redly blushing cheeks and scarlet mouths. The ladies usually sported garishly-coloured bows in their hair, while the mens' hair was sleekly brilliantined. I loved the men best, becoming passionately fond of Stewart Granger. He was my first 'crush', the first man to haunt my dreams, enfolding me in his strong arms, looking lovingly upon me with dark lustrous eyes.

Collecting bus tickets became a ruling passion after Keith and I heard from a friend that some of the tickets bore 'Lucky Numbers' that could, if found, win us a fortune. We spent hours haunting the bus terminus and dredging the gutters for tickets, which we stuffed in our coat pockets and sorted out in the garden shed. We knew better than to take them into the house as mom had warned us about our ticket-collecting.

'You ain't bringin' them dairty things in this 'ouse. It'll be who'd uv thought it if yer end up wiv scarlit fever in the Isolation 'ospital. Mark me werds'.

As usual mom's dire warnings fell upon deaf ears. We had so many hidings for things we couldn't help doing wrong there seemed little point in heeding her threats. And we both knew that if we got scarlet fever we would be cosseted and sent to the Open Air School which catered for children with tuberculosis and other such debilitating ailments. There they lay out in beds in the lovely grounds of the school and there was, we were told, a sliding roof above their classrooms so that when the sun shone they could sit at their desks with only the sky above them. It sounded much more fun than our boring old school.

'Wot ya gonna do wiv the money if ya win it our Joanny'?, asked Keith time and again, as we searched our hoards of grubby tickets spread out over the shed floor.

'I ain't quite med me mind up yet. Wouldn't our mom be 'appy if we did win? First thing I'd do is buy 'er a fur coat like wot that Greta Garbo wore in that film, yer know, 'er was a Queen or Princess or somat. An' I'd gerr 'er some new teeth and tek 'er to 'ave 'er 'air pairmed like Betty Grable . . .'

'Betty Grable's got yeller 'air and our mom's got brown 'air, our Joanny'.

'Well, like Rosalind Russell's then. An' I'd 'ave a coat an' bonnit with flowers round the brim like Princess Margaret Rose wears, an' black patent shoes with silver buckles. An' then I'd buy us a big 'ouse up the Broadway by the 'King George', ya know, where our Sunday School teacher lives. An' we'd 'ave red carpets an' blazin' log fires an' four poster beds an' everythin' . . . an' me an' you'll 'ave a big sledge pulled by black 'orses for when it snows . . .' I could see it all, smell the logs burning, the lavender-scented drapes around the bed, hear the tinkle of the sleigh bells . . .

'Wot about the Old Mon then?'

'Blow 'im our Keith. 'E can tek 'is 'ook. Goo off with one of 'is wimin. 'E aint comin' to stink my 'ouse out . . . I wouldn't gie 'im nuthin', norr even if 'e begged me on 'is knees . . .' I was prevented from elaborating further when tears pricked the back of my eyes.

'But wor if our dad says 'e's sorry an' 'e's nice to ya when you'm rich?'

Damn, I hadn't thought of that. Gazing unseeing at the shed walls I saw my father stroking my hair, felt his soft fatherly hand upon my head, saw him smiling without mockery as Shirley Temple's father had done only last week at the pictures. I had prayed to God for a miracle to happen and make my dad love me and be proud of me. But no, it wouldn't be any good if he only loved me because I'd got money.

'No Keith, if 'e's only nice to me 'cos of the money 'e needn't bother.' I tried to harden my heart as I saw him rapping on the oak door of the big house on Broadway. He was begging me to let him in out of the snow. I gazed at him through the leaded panes of the window in an agony of indecision . . .

'Wot ya cryin' for Joanny? Yer tickets'll be sobbin' wet'.

'Tain't nuthin . . . Oh Keith, I just 'ATE BEIN' POOR'.

After I'd stopped wailing we carried on sorting out our tickets in silence for some time.

'If I win . . .' Keith interrupted my reverie. 'I'm gonna buy an airoplane, like Biggles 'as, an' I'm gonna fly round the world. Ya can cum wiv me . . .' And so we spent many, many such hours sorting and sifting our tickets and our dreams. And, best of all, at any moment our dreams might become reality.

Sometimes I joined Keith and his friends in Train Spotting down by the railway junction. Here we took notes of the names and numbers of the gleaming steam trains and argued the toss about whether or not we had 'had' that particular train before. There were proper books you could buy which listed all the details of every train on the railways, but we never managed to afford such a book. Our records, kept on odd bits of paper, were always being burned by mom because we had no proper place to keep our few possessions.

When we were older Josy deigned to take me with her on some of her sketching expeditions after Margaret started to spend more time away from home with her best friend. She had a favourite spot, hidden in a hollow beside the railway siding, where Weeping Willows lazily fingered the murky stream. We sat high above the water in the cleft of two big branches, our sketch pads resting against a gnarled flattened branch growing at a convenient angle.

These rare excursions stand out, for me, like bright cameos. Whilst my sister laboriously sketched the wild flowers that rioted at the river's edge, I lost myself in what I came to call my 'green dreams'. I felt as one with the tree trunk, felt its living breathing presence blend with mine. Sunlight, sparkling and bouncing off the water, shimmered amongst the green almost translucent leaves that surrounded me. A throbbing, glowing sensation pervaded my whole body and my spirit transcended into some mystical world of one-ness.

I experienced the same phenomenon sometimes upon first surveying 'our' fields over the common land near the canal, after being absent all winter. Suddenly I would feel the grass 'breathing': grass and sky, birdsong and Buttercups merged with my own self in an unearthly one-ness, a bright, harmonious whole. The feeling only lasted a few timeless moments. These rare experiences, about which I was wholly inarticulate, served later to enhance the ugliness of my home surroundings and caused my spirit to rage in impotent, mute despair. I felt like a trapped animal, mentally beating the bars of my cage until my grief was spent and the blessed amnesia and optimism of childhood restored, once more, a precarious balance.

Later, in early adolescence, Josy introduced me to a less innocent game called 'Truth, Dare, Kiss or Promise'. We played this game in the winter under the gas lamps, a few streets away from Shelley Road, or in the gloomy dark depths of an old Air Raid Shelter. Boys from Josy's Grammar School flocked on bicycles to this venue, attracted to our beautiful Josy like bees round a honey-pot. Many of them were two or three years older than me and already had shadowy moustaches and broken voices.

I was very shy with 'big' boys and blushed easily, paralysed with fear and excitement when one of the better-looking boys must kiss me for a penalty. Usually these kisses were pecks on the cheek, but one night an older boy gave me an adult, passionate kiss, up the corner of the air-raid shelter. The world turned upside down and I saw flashing, sparkling fireworks. It was the nearest I ever came to fainting in my whole life. I was terrified of my reaction and never played with the gang again. At fourteen I was too old for street games, and too young to wish to join in more adult pastimes.

CHAPTER FOURTEEN

# Paper Dolls and Other Games.

Margaret organised our play on wet or wintry days when we could not play out of doors. Seated around the chipped enamel-topped kitchen table beside the gas stove we waited expectantly for big sister to weave her magic and alleviate our boredom.

Carefully she mixed together plain flour and water to a proper gluey consistency, having already distributed old newspapers for shredding into small pieces. Soon we were deeply and messily absorbed in the delights of papier-mâché. Margaret's and Josy's puppet-heads quickly became recognisable as Punch or Judy, while the beautiful doll's head I was attempting to fashion stayed stubbornly in the mind's eye alone. The boys usually contented themselves with simply rolling the soggy mess into marbles or balls, to be later painted in lurid colours.

Flour paste was also used for sticking cut-out pictures onto sheets of newspapers to make 'scrap books'. With only one blunt rusty pair of scissors between us, we had to wait our turn to cut out interesting illustrations from the old magazines and mail-order catalogues Margaret collected from goodness-knew-where.

Margaret always had a store of typing paper, carbon paper, pencils, folders and bull-dog clips that she had nagged dad into bringing home from his office. It was sheer magic to trace a picture in a magazine and find it exactly reproduced on blank paper when we removed the carbon.

From tracing it was a natural step to begin drawing free-hand, at which Josy excelled from the earliest age. How I envied her this gift as I sought unsuccessfully to imitate her efforts, or to create pictures out of my imagination. I knew I was good at drawing, but had not the patience to be as accurate or precise as Josy. Yet it was I who sold my paintings when I was grown up, and Josy admitted that as a child she had envied me my imaginative flair.

Margaret owned a beautiful large doll called Elizabeth. With white china complexion, blushing cheeks and improbably blue eyes, Elizabeth was as remote and untouchable as an angel. She lay coffined in tissue-paper in a box beside Margaret's bed, and big sister DARED us to touch her. We didn't. Elizabeth's origins were shrouded in mystery. Margaret told us that, during the war, dad had taken her on a long train journey to the sea-side. Here she had stayed with a kind lady for a few weeks, sleeping in a pretty bed, lulled to sleep by the crashing of waves on the rocks below the bedroom window. The lady had cried when Margaret had to return home and had presented her with Elizabeth to remember her by. Years later we realised that this lady had been dad's sweetheart during the war, the woman who had been the love of his life and whom he had renounced in order to return to his wife and children.

For a brief period Josy and I had owned identical dolls with cheap crock heads and sawdust-filled bodies. One sad day I stole, with the 'twins', into the bathroom, and there filled the sink with hot sudsy water to bath the beloved pair. I wanted to surprise Josy with a clean, sparkling doll, then maybe she would play nicely with me and be my friend forever. Enthusiastically I dunked the pair up and down in the water, lathering them copiously with Sunlight soap.

Alas, the end was tragic. Alerted by my unusual silence mom surprised me, engrossed as I was in my task. After giving me a thorough hiding she placed the dolls on the rack above the fire, where they dripped sawdust and glue for days, ruined beyond recall, their faces shapeless lumps streaked with paint. They were ceremonially buried in the garden, sharing a cardboard coffin. Margaret officiated, organising our prayers and hymns, after which the mourners scattered wild flowers and tears on the filled-in grave. Josy never did forgive me, or become my friend.

The only other cuddly toys were a thread-bare head-less

Teddy communally shared, and Josy's beloved hand-knitted doll called Nitty that had been made for her by a school friend's mother. Josy guarded Nitty jealously and threatened me with physical violence if I should touch her beloved doll.

We jointly possessed a few beautifully illustrated books gifted to us by Granny Stafford. These books were carefully hoarded by Margaret, who brought them down to the living room on dull days and shared with us their heady delights. At her knee we learned about the Knights of the Round Table, the adventures of the Swiss Family Robinson and the beautiful tales of Hans Christian Anderson. For years they were inextricably mixed up in my imagination.

For us three girls our favourite game was undoubtedly Paper Dolls. It was played in our 'big' bedroom, Margaret and Josy playing their game jointly at one end of the room, whilst I played in happy isolation, for once, in 'my half'. We were the teachers and our cut-out paper dolls were the pupils. Classrooms were, for my sisters, made up of father's books standing on the bare floorboards in squares and forming partitions. My class-rooms were usually set out along the window-ledge which was low and wide.

Our pupils were children cut out of magazines and catalogues, each child carefully chosen for its likeness to one or two others representing children of the same family who attended our schools. On the reverse of each figure we neatly wrote the child's name, age and relationship to other pupils in different classes. We each kept a Register listing their details and names in alphabetical order. Each doll was neatly folded at the waist to enable it to sit up.

The naming of these children was undertaken with great care and required much reference to books Margaret had borrowed from the library. In the early days of paper dolls Margaret was in her 'Scottish' phase and the pupils' names mirrored this preoccupation.

While playing this game we three girls lived in a totally imaginary world peopled with magnificent Highland Lairds and their equally splendid Ladies, eternally dressed in full Highland regalia. The handsome, claymore-wielding, bonneted Lairds regularly swept down from their remote turreted castles to visit our schools, leaving behind mountain crags, wheeling golden eagles and furiously-rutting deer. Entering our classrooms with a swirl of heather-scented kilts they would examine the children in their spelling and times tables and inspect the Attendance Records.

In the lulls between these frequent interruptions we teachers had our hands full, keeping our classes of recalcitrant children in order. A pencil would be wielded as a blackboard pointer, or rapped peremptorily on the floorboards calling the pupils to order. Children from castle and croft sat side by side and we teachers knew the characteristics of each one, having a goodly sprinkling of Rebels and Favourites.

'Morag, do sit down. No Hamish, ye may not leave the room, ye've been twice this morning already. Good gracious, McFarlane, have ye no handkerchief to blow your nose? Do stop DREAMING Fiona and attend to your lessons. Oh thank you, Jamie dear. Remind me to tell your dear father what an excellent scholar you are when next he honours us with his presence . . .' For hours upon end we girls were lost in the misty Highlands, escaping through the tunnel of our imagination into a world of wild forests and craggy mist-covered mountains, fresh, heather-scented air, haunting bagpipes and aromatic peat fires.

Paper Dolls became a major part of our lives, the game growing and extending in our imagination and continuing well into early adolescence. When Margaret's reading moved into the 'Irish' phase we transferred our classrooms to Bantry Bay, where our children were barefoot Roisins Colleens and Bridgits, Seans Padraics and Kierans. These pupils lived out their lives knee-deep in Irish peat bogs, their conversation dripping with blarney.

The shock of mother's voice shouting from the bottom of the stairs never ceased to hurt somewhere deep inside.

'Cum on, yow gairls. Ya tea's gooing cold. I've called ya three tymes already'

My Celtic School abruptly faded and the dreary bedroom emerged with its skimped faded curtains and plaster-peeling walls. Pins and needles attacked my feet upon rising from a kneeling position before the window, and as the soft mists cleared I saw my pupils for what they were. Just paper cut-outs lining the window-ledge. No soft Island or Highland mist either, just dirty rivulets of Midlands rain running down the window panes. Once again I was plain Joanny, and the knowledge was almost too much to bear as I reluctantly trudged downstairs with my sisters.

Birthday Cards was another game for inclement weather. Over the years Margaret collected cards from various sources, to be produced when boredom threatened. Birthday cards in those days were generally highly coloured glossy post-cards, with grossly sentimental verses printed on them in extravagantly flourishing lettering. They usually had a border of embossed dimples or scrolls, and often depicted riotously-flowering gardens. Most of these gardens boasted rose arbours and pristine lawns dotted with sundials and fountains. Other cards pictured coy persian cats in baskets with large satin bows at their throats. My favourite cards, however, were the ones with 'the Ladies' depicted on them, their expressions even more coy than the kittens. They had improbable coiffures and elongated swan-like necks. Blood-red cupid-bow lips either pouted provocatively or smiled winsomely, revealing snow-white perfect teeth. And Oh, their dresses! Beautiful pastel coloured tea-gowns, soft and silky, draping in becoming folds across gently swelling bosoms with perhaps a full-blown rose tucked into a discreet cleavage. There were definitely no ladies like those on Greenpark Estate. Margaret, who knew everything, said they were 'London Ladies', and I determined to join their ranks when I grew up. Somehow, some Fairy Godmother would magic away my physical imperfections.

For the playing of the Birthday Card game Margaret shuffled the cards, selecting one to hide behind her back. We children then took turns at guessing which particular card she was hiding, knowing each card in the most minute detail. The child who guessed correctly became the next shuffler.

Father introduced Margaret to the game of Battleships. He obtained graph paper on which to draw up their individual games. After numbering the squares alphabetically and numerically, each player marked boldly, on their own sheet, the symbolised Battleships, Cruisers, Submarines and Tug-boats. Much to father's proud delight Margaret showed great cunning and skill in this game.

She introduced us younger ones to the delights of Battleships. On wet days the living room rang with cries of 'A.4.' 'Missed. Your turn'. 'G.7.' 'Missed. Your turn'. 'A.5.' 'Blow it. You've 'it one of me submarines'.

In such games we honed our wits for the battles ahead and enjoyed ourselves enormously, too.

Father, in a rare flash of parental enthusiasm, or perhaps conscience, installed an old coke-burning stove in the wooden garden shed. For a few brief months we inhabited this rough-and-ready playroom, playing our games at a roughly knocked-up table. Or, huddled cosily around the stove, we listened spellbound while Margaret told us ghost stories as the wind and rain battered at the flimsy building. All too soon our cosy home was lost to us when father entered his gardening phase, and later his hen phase. The shed was never the same again.

CHAPTER FIFTEEN

# Social Changes.

Nurse Barratt was present at every confinement in our area. A small, bustling, blue-clad body, even her hair beneath her black felt hat seemed starched. The appearance of her sit-up-and-beg bicycle at a neighbour's gate confirmed, for Keith and me, what we had already gleaned from neighbours' whispered asides and silent-mouthed conversations over the palings.

After the birth was completed Nurse Barratt held court. Black bag clutched to her prim spinster bosom, she regaled the gathered crowd with every gory detail of the birth. It was entirely unethical and wholly entertaining. To be on the fringes of one of these 'conflabs', securely hidden behind some ample bottom, was to know nature in the raw. Here Keith and I learned of breech-birth, after-birth, prolonged labour, inverted nipples, prolapses, still-births and deformities. We also learned Nurse Barratt's personal views on courage and cowardice.

Here began, for me, a life-long horror of child-birth and an awareness of the desperate need for birth control. Regrettably, the Nurse's lurid accounts of travail and torture obviously fell upon deafer adult ears, for our neighbours continued to breed like proverbial rabbits. It was some years before I realised the part men played in conception, despite much deep speculation between Keith and myself, leading us to some pretty surprising conclusions all extremely wide of the mark.

Funerals, too, were a good source of education and entertainment. Each neighbourhood had its own resident layer-out. Ours was Mrs Gosling, a witch-like shapeless old

hag with a wispy white moustache and dirty long finger-
nails, leaving one to speculate on the ultimate cleanliness of
the corpse. She, too, held court after each laying out, each
aspect of the corpse being described in fascinating sickening
detail.

Here Keith and I learned how the bundle of cotton-wool
she invariably carried was used to best purpose, of death-
rattles and rigor mortis. We learned of sightless eyes that
refused to stay shut despite the judicious application of old
pennies, and of the difficulties encountered in dressing
corpses whose limbs would not straighten, and the necessary breaking of such bones.

A door-to-door collection was carried out immediately
after the death by the nearest of the deceased's neighbours.
The collected money would be used to buy a large wreath
for the funeral, and to insert a fulsome verse in the 'Walsall
Observer'. The paper had stock verses to choose from,
usually on the lines of one that has lodged in my memory:-
"God felt the rugged pathway
Was getting hard to climb.
He gently closed your weary eyes,
And whispered 'Peace be Thine'".

It didn't matter whether the deceased was a saint or a
sinner, there would still be a sentimental verse in the paper
followed by 'sadly missed by your neighbours at Shelley
Road'. It was a favourite pastime of Keith and myself to read
aloud to each other the columns of verses under 'Deaths'.
The maudling sentiments and trite verses reduced us to
hysterical wrecks within minutes, tears of wild mirth
streaming down our faces.

No-one dared to refuse a generous donation towards a
'mark of respect'. Each family was well aware that it might
be their turn next, and it was everyone's deep wish not to
get themselves talked about by neighbours.

Even the poorest families carried simple Death Insurance,
the Insurance man or lady being familiar visitors to our
homes as they called to collect weekly payments from each
family. After a death there would be much ripe speculation
among neighbourhood gossips as to how much Insurance
Money would be paid out, and on what it would be spent.

Before the funeral, bodies were usually kept in the living room. This must have caused much inconvenience to the household as this was the only room downstairs except for the small kitchen. Perhaps this was to facilitate the removal of the body to the hearse, as the staircases of these houses were narrow and 'L' shaped. The curtains of the room would remain drawn from the time of death until the burial. All the neighbours drew their curtains about half an hour before the hearse arrived, as a 'mark of respect'. I recall my mother drawing the curtains during the war, shutting out a lovely sunny day. In response to my query she told me her brother had been killed 'over Italy'. His body was never recovered yet still the custom must be observed, indicating her bereavement to neighbours.

A hearse was always provided, even for the tiniest baby, the Undertakers mute and solemn in unrelieved black serge suits and top hats acting as Bearers. Often the hearse and coffin were all that could be afforded, leaving black-clad relatives to make their own way by bus or on foot to church and cemetery.

Cremation was almost unheard of in those days, and after the funeral relatives seemed to find much comfort in visiting the grave-side, bearing bunches of cut-flowers they could ill-afford, at least once a week. Grief was something to be publicly displayed, and deep mourning went on for quite some time after bereavement. Close family wore black arm-bands, if they could not afford 'full black' during the lengthy period of mourning, a visual sign indicating vulnerability and need for consolation. Valium had not yet been invented and nature was allowed to take its course.

Weddings were less obviously celebrated, in general, brides usually being well on in pregnancy. With money urgently needed for midwife and pram there was little to spare for finery. Clothes were still on coupons for some time after the war ended, and the wedding outfit for the bus trip to church or Registry Office usually consisted of borrowed frock or costume (two piece suit), hat and court shoes. A fur tippet would be worn if the bride was able to borrow one from a better-off relative.

In later years the date of the marriage would be conveniently altered to nine months before the birth of the first-born. Illegitimate births were rare, most girls having gangs of tough brothers and uncles who could be relied upon to lean heavily on any prospective escapees. I recall vividly seeing one such unwilling bridegroom quite brutally done over, just outside our house. Despite a large crowd of gathered neighbours who regularly witnessed such fights, no one would have dared to call the police. Such were the boy's injuries on this occasion that someone did find a telephone box and send for an ambulance, but no charges were brought and the marriage was duly solemnised. Rumour was rife that this lad would never father children again, so perhaps it was no coincidence that there was only one child of that marriage.

Another integral part of our community were 'the Dafties'. Every street had at least one. Shelley Road boasted Big Georgie, a large, shambling, vacant albino. Wreathed in perpetual smiles, Georgie shunted himself tirelessly round and round our block of council houses, making 'chuff chuff' noises, driving his arms around rythmically like train wheels. When crossing the road to take in the next block he waved an imaginary flag and emitted an ear-piercing whistle.

Whenever we saw him we would chant "Georgie Porgie Pudden' and Pie. Kissed the girls and made them cry . . ." Georgie paid no heed whatsoever intent as he was, perhaps, on keeping his train to a time-table. Or was he simply deaf? Beautifully cared for and dearly loved by his family, an eternal six-foot three-year-old, he enriched our lives with his beaming innocence. One morning he simply failed to wake up, and was much grieved over and sadly missed.

Rumour had it that Big Georgie was secretly courting Daft Mary, the next street's resident idiot. She was a large bovine girl with a cruel squint and greasy shoulder-length, lank hair. Not so well-kept as Georgie, Mary wore a shapeless faded print dress, winter and summer, and baggy hand-knitted stretched cardigan. Georgie and Mary were often to be seen deep in 'conversation' with each other, emitting funny noises, gesticulating and laughing up-roariously, entirely oblivious of anything except each other.

Doubtless they could have taught us all a lesson in true love.

In the neighbourhood of Shelley Road it was general knowledge that both these unfortunates had been dropped on their heads in infancy, as had one of my cousins on mother's side who was certainly not 'all there'. I was so glad our mom had not been so careless.

Nowadays those two free spirits would have been Institutionalised, living out their lives behind locked doors, drugged up to the eye balls. As unthinkable, when we were young, as caging a nightingale. These 'different' people enhanced our lives, added colour to the local landscape, and were an integral part of the caring community which could accommodate the halt and the lame along with the so-called whole.

In later years most of the Shelley Road neighbours were pressured to move into high-rise flats scattered around Walsall, after their children were grown and their houses deemed 'too large' for them. I visit some of them still. In general they are isolated and unhappy, sadly bewailing the loss of contact and continuity with their erstwhile neighbours. The Planners called it progress.

CHAPTER SIXTEEN

# The New Garden.

Father's squad of labourers, delegated to carry out his grandiose scheme for the new garden, was soon reduced by two. Margaret and Josy went Absent Without Leave – as usual. They had learned early how to gang up on the enemy and were skilled in evading the consequences of their actions. Their intelligent cunning amused father and he dealt lightly with them.

Keith and I were slow learners and dad despised our apparent lack of intelligence. We were the Rookies of father's army – fit only to wield shovels and dig trenches. For weeks we worked like a pair of yoked oxen. We didn't mind. We had been promised extra rations and pay, and as we sweated and heaved under the hot sun we shared our dreams of the spending spree we would enjoy when the job was completed.

To be fair dad did dig the garden over, burying the glorious weeds – the erstwhile walls of our separate playrooms. Soon Daisies, Hemlock (which we called 'Naughty Man's Play Thing') purple Willow Herb and Foxgloves lay slain about our feet, their delicate beauty shrivelled and faded. I wish I'd known that they would provide nourishment for the flowers we would soon plant. It would somehow have eased the pain.

What could not be dug in was carted by the Squaddies to the bonfire site in the side garden. Seeing how slowly we worked dad constructed a wheelbarrow out of the inverted top of an old cabinet, two lengths of wood for handles, and two pram wheels, which proved crude but effective. Father's other carpentry contribution to the new garden was the construction of a rough wooden seat placed beneath the living room window, facing the new garden. When he had finished digging he retired to this seat, his work done. From here he could comfortably direct operations while smoking his pipe and drinking his beer.

To help sustain dad in this arduous task, Keith and I ran in relays to and from the public house on our estate that dad never personally frequented. Right down Shelley Road's steep hill we scurried, four empty screw-top Tizer bottles rattling in the shopping bag against our legs, precious coins clutched tightly in our tight fists. Into the 'Out Door', standing tip-toe at the bar, arms outstretched above our heads proferring the money, we gasped at the unseen barman.

'Two pints of draught mild and two pints of draught bitter, please sir'.

We would hear the beer hissing, hear the pump being pulled, the jug filling and frothing. Then the 'glug' as it was decanted into the empty bottles. Out of the pub, bag heavy now, the journey to Shelley Road much longer. How steep seemed the hill now as we toiled to the house on the top corner. Keith and I would separately run this errand two times each during the course of the morning and early afternoon, to quench dad's thirst. At 1.o'clock dad would walk the mile to a canal-side pub with Dog, leaving us to carry on with our work. Back he would come at three o'clock, go to bed for a couple of hours, then direct our labours once more from his seat until opening time at six.

Our first task was to break up the soil and barrow the half-end-duckers and sundry stones to the rubbish heap, along with 'switch' which, I think, was Ground Elder and Convolvulus. I loved the white trumpets that peeped out from the shiny green Ivy leaves and felt sad and guilty as I tore out their roots, watching them crumple and die under the pitiless sun. Slowly we worked our way through the garden, gleefully demolishing Josy's worm and caterpillar hospital. Together we worked as a team, chatting companionably or singing the hymns we had learned almost before we could talk from our evangelical Sunday School.

Dad made us feel important by showing us his sketches of

the garden as he envisaged it. Happy were we to help construct this 'Jacob's Ladder', seeing it all in our minds' Dad was a superb artist and Keith and I, gifted with great imagination, were able to share his dream. Not strange, then, that Keith and I should both grow up to be competent gardeners.

Our garden described an elongated arc, walled all around. Flowerbeds were to be under the window flanking dad's seat. An herbaceous border was to run all around the outside of the lawns, which would run the length of the garden. Just further than centre of the lawns would be a large flowerbed in which would also be planted trees, mainly Weeping Willows that dad had spotted growing down at the Sewage Farm. Shrubs would be planted at the back of the herbaceous border, to grow tall and shield the garden from prying eyes.

In broad daylight father took us on a Reccy to the new school gardens and pointed out his choice of shrubs. Carefully we noted the whereabouts of Laburnum, Flowering Cherry, Flowering Currant, Laurel and Golden Privet. Then he led us along the road on a Route March to observe where council workmen were laying a new road. We noted broken paving slabs and gravel. Father explained that these operations must be carried out under cover of darkness, with the aid of the wheelbarrow. We would receive danger money at the rate of two-pence half-penny per barrowload. Daredevils that we were, and budding entrepreneurs to boot, we willingly agreed that, should we get caught, we would not reveal our Captain's part in the operation. More scared of dad than any flat-footed policeman on the beat we well knew which side our bread was buttered.

Father's Master Plan included crazy paving paths running up the centre of the lawn and looping around the centre-piece. Also paths were to run among the flowerbeds beneath the window. It all added up to a lot of broken slabs and gravel. With optimism borne of youth and ignorance Keith and I set to. Night after exhausting night we dragged our barrow up Shelley Road, walking backwards, each pulling a handle. Scraggy arms aching almost beyond endurance, we rested by sitting on the pavement when we had the stitch in our sides. Our fingers were bleeding and torn with the rough stones. Still we laboured, carefully noting how many barrowloads we had shifted. Dad explained that we couldn't be paid until the paths were laid, good-naturedly showing us how to prepare the 'bed' first and then 'key-in' the stones with the minimum space between them. The gravel was to go in these spaces. Back dad went to his seat, and day after day we toiled on hands and knees our hair bleached white by the summer sun, our faces, arms and bare legs sunburned and tender.

From the market dad purchased grass-seed, having failed to locate a source of ready-made turf we could dig up. He had turned the shed into a greenhouse, filling old wax gramophone records he had heated and moulded into flower pots with Lupin seeds, Pansies and the aptly-named Love Lies Bleeding. They flourished under his inexpert green fingers, to be planted out around the borders.

The shrubs and trees flourished, despite our crude cutting of roots with hasty spade-work. Five Weeping Willows were planted in the centre bed, to be watered twice daily by Keith and I, along with the shrubs in front of the walls and all the new plants. The plants were watered using a cocoa tin with holes punched in the bottom, dipped into a bucket and sprinkled over the flowers. This was the task I enjoyed most watching the droplets of water, rainbow-hued as they fell, caught like crystals in the centre of the Lupin leaves or starring the bright faces of the Pansies. I did not enjoy carting the full bucket of water up the garden time after tiring time.

In a bed beneath the window dad had sown Night Scented Stock and it was heavenly, on hot summer evenings, to lean out of our open bedroom window and smell the glorious perfume wafting up on the still night air. How good to watch the moths flit and dance above the flowers, when the living room light went on below our window. Hour upon hour, it seems, I leaned out of the casement window, dad absent from his seat, Josy and Margaret elsewhere. It was balm to the spirit, food for the hungry soul starved of beauty and blessed solitude.

I loved to walk round the garden after rain, smelling the

'tom-cat' smell of the Flowering Currants, watching the water drip from the delicate willow-leaves as they hung their hair out to dry in the breeze. How sorry I felt for mother at such times, unable to smell the wet grass, the damp earth, the flowers and trees. But a fall in childhood had robbed her of this sense and she would never regain it. Poor mom. It would have been worse, for me, than being deprived of food or clothing. It was only a small blessing that she couldn't smell dad farting or unwashed bodies and sweaty armpits, and of course our lavvy.

As the Willows grew, rapidly as is their wont, dad ran a cable from the hall light socket up the garden to the centre of the trees. He halved a cocoa tin and made a crude cradle for the 100 watt light bulb which he placed among the Willows. After the pub had closed, on hot summer evenings he sat on his bench smoking his pipe, lord of all he surveyed. Through alcohol-tinted spectacles he proudly drank in the beauty of 'his' illuminated garden, quietly watching the fronds of Willows finger the night air in lacy beauty.

At such times did he dream of the girl he had left behind in that seaside place after the war? Did he dream of a world far away from Shelley Road, clean and sweet-smelling? Did he grieve for what-might-have-been, had Fate taken a different turn? Dealt him a better hand? He never said and we would never know. Only once, when Margaret left her first husband for another man, did he mention his own sacrifice. 'I could have gone off with another woman and left you kids. Think of your children', he counselled her. Margaret replied, in her straight-forward manner, that if she stayed with her husband she 'might make as bad a job of things as dad had'. Happily for her she took another bite at the cherry and found it sweet.

The Willow trees grew to almost over-top the house, forming shady green arches either side of the lawn and shielding us from the public gaze. Neighbours lurching home from the pub, thinking themselves unheard, leaned on the wall the better to admire the lit-up Willows.

'Ain't it luvly, our Bill. It's just like the H'Illuminations at The Arboretum, ain'it. Yow wouldn't think yow was in Shelley Road would ya? More like Bucking'am Palace'.

'Ey. yow'm right, our Syd. That bloody Stafford chap must be good at summat'.

'That bleedin' penpusher? Never done an 'ard days wear in 'is life. Them kids done it, dain't they? Poor likkle buggers'. Dad sat and sipped his beer, laughing softly to himself at the ignorance of the local peasantry.

We all enjoyed the garden, really. Margaret and Josy lay on the grass under the Willows, reading their books. I picked and pressed Pansies in my Sunday School Prize Bible, or lay watching the bees and butterflies, thinking. Always thinking, endlessly taking things out of the attic of my mind, puzzling over them, then stuffing them back. I never seemed to be able to close the door firmly on the collected jumble. That was the trouble with me. It took half a lifetime to learn to throw out the rubbish, to finally make everything reasonably sweet and clean. One has to learn to live, amicably, with the unwanted mental furniture that is bolted securely to the floor, contenting oneself with fitting new covers and scattering around pretty ornaments and posies to hide the blemishes. Luckily, for me, there are always the gardens of the mind, past, present and still to come. A gardener will always have a 'Jacob's Ladder' to climb in happy anticipation.

Of course Keith and I had the upkeep of the garden as a continuing chore. Cutting grass with blunt shears, weeding and hoeing in between flowers and pulling grass up from between the crazy-paving-stones. We received no extra pocket money or favours, knowing full well what we'd get from dad if we neglected to perform our chores. The truce with father had only lasted for the duration of the construction of the new garden. Immediately afterwards pleasantries ceased and total hostility resumed.

What did Keith and I do with the extra money we earned for our hard labours in the garden? After waiting a seemly interval we jointly approached dad with an outright request. We each presented him with a bill itemising each barrowload, each bill totalling twelve shillings and sixpence.

'As much as that?' Dad's voice registered feigned shock and surprise. He was seated on his bench beneath the window, enjoying his pint, braces dangling down the sides of his trousers, beer belly hanging over his belt. Still loosely handsome, in a seedy Dylan Thomas way with brown curly hair falling over his fine forehead, his blue eyes twinkled at us for a moment, amused at our temerity. After an exaggerated pause he said solemnly.

'That money's in the bank'.

'What bank?' we cried in unison.

'The bank that's got handles on the bank books'. He threw back his head and roared with laughter, revelling unashamedly in our slowly dawning horror. Keith and I knew better than to argue. Tails between our legs we slunk away, feeling cheated and murderous, kicking ourselves for our stupidity. Once again we were the victims of one of dad's 'little jokes'. Keith was wearing a green tie with a yellow stripe running through it. Father's parting shot was perfectly timed for maximum effect. 'And I'd get that bloody tie off if I were you. It's quite sufficient having a yellow belly without having a matching stripe across what is laughingly called your chest'. Once again we were the victims of one of dad's 'little jokes'. It took us a long time to learn, Keith and I.

## CHAPTER SEVENTEEN

# Learning Lessons.

It is, perhaps, an exaggeration to state that what I learned during formal education could be written on the reverse of a postage stamp, but a foolscap sheet might suffice.

At Infant School I learned to read and write, to chant times tables and to knit both plain and purl. Most of our teachers were war time conscripts brought out of retirement for the Duration; they were 'Misses' of great age and greater strictness and cruelty, beating lessons into us with the aid of a black-board pointer wielded with malice and afore-thought. Wooden rulers were also regularly rapped hard across baby-soft knuckles. The effect of this treatment was entirely predictable, and to this day I loathe knitting only slightly less than mathematics. The seven-times-table refused to stay in my brain, and long division was the final hurdle at which I fell. It must be admitted that I have never felt unduly deprived by an inability to knit or do sums.

It was, however, my great good fortune that no Virago in all her fury could quench my thirst for, or love of, the English language. I positively shone at spelling and reading. To be given an essay to write in class was to escape into another world. Being forever told that I was 'far too imaginative for my own good', I now began to use this questionable asset. Choosing the most obscure title off I went, pencil scurrying across the flimsy, war-issue jotter, head held inches from the page. With glasses usually broken, I had just begun to realise how limited was my vision. Teacher didn't, deeming it necessary to yank my head back by the hair in a vain attempt to improve my slovenly posture. I felt no pain, mind soaring out of the window, boredom abated.

Teacher's sharp 'Pencils down' reached me from far away. I wished to stay forever in that dream-state, content and free. A flying missile of chalk brought me back to earth. Days later the jotters would be returned duly marked, and all through my schooling I rarely received less than eight, nine or ten marks out of ten, minus five for bad hand-writing. Almost every School Report states 'Has ability but will not use it. Careless, untidy worker'.

After Greenpark Infants came Blackhouse Junior School, a grim Victorian building half way to Walsall. Teachers were quick to realise that I was not in the mould of my studious older sisters, never tiring of holding up their bright academic achievements with sickening regularity. 'How', queried a succession of teachers, 'could two such paragons of learning come to have such an untidy, careless, lazy sister?' My brothers, coming after me, fared a little better by my abysmal example.

Both sisters passed the eleven-plus. Margaret left to attend the new Greenpark Secondary Modern Comprehen-sive School. She stayed on at school until she was sixteen, becoming a star pupil and prefect, and taking her 'O' levels. She must have been the first child on our estate to receive Higher Education, but there was no chance of her going on to University. She must become a wage earner as quickly as possible.

Josy won a coveted scholarship to Walsall's Grammar School, where wealthy parents could still buy a place for their children if they failed the eleven-plus. Poor Josy, she might have done well had she not laboured from the beginning under a dreadful handicap, namely our dad. How proud he had been when his favourite, golden-curled, clever daughter won the same scholarship as had he in his youth. In those days it was simply not possible for slum children to take their place there. The uniform was flam-boyant and expensive, and one must possess one's own tennis racket, hockey stick etc., together with a host of incidentals.

However Josy did not have to worry about such things, for well she knew that father was entitled to a Government

Grant on her behalf. Twenty whole pounds was duly
granted and Josy trusted dad to take her on a shopping
expedition before term began. Her trust was misplaced.
The Grant was in his name, and he spent the lot.

She therefore began her new school under a severe
handicap. She only possessed half of the uniform and had no
idea when she would obtain the rest. With the aid of a hastily
acquired Provident Cheque, to be repaid by mother at ten
shillings a week, a mackintosh, a blazer, Tam-o-shanter and
navy school satchel were purchased. Over the next three
years Josy gradually acquired a few second-hand items of
uniform, regularly skipping classes through lack of sports
gear or text books, losing House Points and dignity at every
turn.

It was an unhappy experience for her and was not made
any easier by having to run the gauntlet, daily, of the local
rabble as she progressed in stately fashion to and from the
bus, head in air. I regret to state that I joined in the cat-calls
and jeers. I, too, bitterly resented her airs and graces. Or
was I jealous?

Josy left school a few weeks before her fifteenth birthday
under a large cloud. Father had a good position as Works
Manager in a large Engineering firm. He was also in charge
of Book-Keeping, being extraordinarily clever with
figures. Over the years he had perfected, he thought, a
system of fraudulent entries and was pocketing an extra
weekly wage-packet. The books were audited annually and
all seemed well. Eventually the day came when a pimply
callow Accountant, busy with his new broom, queried
these entries and dad was sacked on the spot.

'Father Embezzles for Children' screamed the headline of
the 'Walsall Observer' when the case came to Court. Father
escaped a jail sentence, receiving only a minimum fine and
Probation, when the Judge accepted his plea that he had
been trying to give his children 'a better education than he
could afford'. Of course we never saw a penny of the
money. Josy slunk away from school to become an office
underling.

I failed the eleven-plus. Margaret and Josy had had the
advantage of doing mock exams to prepare for the examina-

tion but as I was in a 'B' stream I was denied such preparation. I finished the paper in fifteen minutes flat, never suspecting there might be trick questions to think about. The questions were so seemingly easy I was sure I'd passed, and was devastated when the results came out. Dad would have thumped me but I managed to lock myself in the bathroom. He shouted through the door what a stupid, good-for-nothing I was and always would be. I screamed back, for once. 'You wait and see. I'll do better than Margaret and Josy'.

After two years in the non-scholarship half of the school Margaret attended, I passed the Examination to Walsall Technical College to the great relief of my teachers. I repeatedly came high in yearly exams and near the bottom in class work, regularly disrupting the class with my clowning and spending most of the lessons outside the door. The only two lessons I excelled at were English and Art and I begged my dad to sign the necessary papers for me to take the Scholarship to the Art College, where I was assured by my teachers of a place. Father said I could only take the examination to the Technical College and 'learn something useful for a change'.

The two years taking the Secretarial Course at the College were a nightmare, and my only ambition from then on was to be an ex-schoolgirl. I hated shorthand and typing only a little less than book-keeping. Our English teacher was a total bore and I even lost interest in that subject, leaving school without knowing a noun from an adjective. Art was not even on the prospectus.

I left school before the end of the term, shortly after my fifteenth birthday, almost entirely ignorant of Music, Poetry, Literature, History, Geography, Maths and Science. I could, however, make a bed with 'hospital corners', boil a four-minute egg, type and write passable shorthand. My spelling had always been excellent, my hand-writing shocking. Armed thus with the little information I had been unable to resist taking on board I stepped out into the world of employment, knowing that shorthand-typists were ten-a-penny and unemployment rife.

Keith and the Babby fared even worse than myself, both

hating school as much as I did. Neither of them even had the opportunity to go to College.

CHAPTER EIGHTEEN

# Evenings At Home.

On cold or wintry evenings we children would race home
from school, to thaw out before the bright fire mom would
have stoked up in readiness for our return.

Tummies full of bread and stew, we lounged contentedly
about the hearth at mom's feet, scratching our chilblains or
heads. The fire cracked and spat out bits of slack and
'batter', the cheapest available fuel. The teapot bubbled on
the hob, stewing the single mash of tea that was all that
could be spared each afternoon, regularly topped up by
boiling water from the kettle that stood beside the teapot.
We always drank Brooke Bond tea because the packet
contained a redeemable penny stamp.

Also on the hob sat the small, waxy tablet of Melrose, for
the annointing of chilblains, giving off it's own peculiar
ointmenty smell. Sometimes there was also the tin of
Kaolin, a white thick substance that smelled of linseed oil.
Spread with a knife onto a piece of lint this was used to
poultice boils and carbuncles.

Our large dog would be sprawled across the hearth,
patiently submitting herself to our enthusiastic embraces,
happily allowing us to remove her fleas which we cracked
between our nails. Cracked fleas gave a satisfying sound we
never tired of hearing. On red-letter days Margaret super-
vised the toasting of bread before the fire, to be spread with
'real' butter, thinly of course.

After we had eaten and settled down around mom's feet
we could sometimes persuade her to get out the photos. Out
of the cupboard beside the fireplace came a biscuit-tin
containing the beloved snap-shots. Sitting in her chair at the

90

fireside, tin on lap, off she went, chanting the litany we never tired of hearing. Speaking in her soft Black Country accent I hear her still, and see her fingers rummaging through the box as she carefully selected photographs and imparted their history.

Sepia images in uniform were our link with the Great War; glossier sharper portraits of uncles in uniform were from the more recent conflict. How handsome they were. Mother gave dark hints of their 'galivantin', which only made them seem more romantic. How proud we were of the uncle who had been reduced to the ranks twice and still left the army highly decorated.

There were many photographs of better-off cousins, all frills and flounces, peering fatly out of posh prams or reclining on studio rugs. There they were again, in crisp sailor suits and Shirley Temple frocks and tresses, simpering against an improbable back-cloth of studio castles and urns. As the poor relations we rarely met these numerous cousins in the flesh, so we just hated and envied them through the medium of photography.

One picture of mother, taken just after she left school at fourteen, was my very favourite. Smiling shyly at the camera, hauntingly beautiful, elfin Greta Garbo face haloed by fashionably permed hair, neck swathed in borrowed fur tippet. Each time I saw this photo I found myself staring up at our mom's lined worn face, broken teeth and straggly hair, chilled and frightened somewhere deep within me at the ravages wrought by child-bearing and poverty, in so few years.

Now father, in soldier's uniform and peaked cap, glanced confidently at the camera, his Sergeant's stripes proudly displayed. He had been a James Mason look-a-like, sensual, brooding and darkly handsome. There was also a tiny snapshot of him in uniform leaning nonchalantly against a garden gate. The woman at his side was represented by only a hint of print dress, for the photograph had been cut down the middle. Was this the Lilian whose name we heard shouted from time to time during arguments, when we were in bed? Lips compressed into a straight line mom said nothing, pushing it quickly to the bottom of the tin.

Margaret and the Babby were the only ones of us who had had their photographs taken in babyhood. Josy and I were photographed together, in a studio, when she was three and my small self two; Josy was all golden curls and immaculate cotton dress, white socks coming neatly to her knees. She looked, as mom said, as if 'butter wouldn't melt in 'er mouth'. I slouched beside her, one chubby hand thrust deep into my crumpled-frock pocket, socks concertina'd into my shoes. My hair was short and straight, scraped up on top in an unbecoming ribbon, my cheeky face screwed up into a broad cross-eyed grin. On the living room wall was a large reproduction of this snapshot, minus me. A few school photographs were the only other record of our growth, together with the single photograph of all five of us taken by a street photographer.

The tin box restored to the cupboard we settled down to listen to 'Children's Hour'. At least the other four children did, while I sat with fingers jammed into my ear-holes. When it was too cold to sit anywhere else in the house I had little alternative, as I could not bear suspense of any kind. The others loved the ghoul-haunted 'Black Abbot' and the fast-moving serials such as 'Dick Barton', but for me 'Worzel Gummage' was the only sort of listening that bore no threat. How the others ragged me for being so yellow bellied. I didn't care, I had enough problems with nightmares without making things worse. I refused to read books for years, for the same reason. Margaret and Josy just couldn't understand me.

Just before the boys' bedtimes, the Babby cradled sleepily on her knee, mom would willingly submit to our request for 'the poems'. She had a limited repertoire, but we never tired of its repetition. 'Meg Merrilies' was chanted in her soft sing-song voice. How well we knew this hardy lady who was 'as brave as Margaret Queen, and tall as Amazon', in her red blanket shawl and chip-hat, secure in her forest home.

"No breakfast had she many a morn,
No dinner many a noon.
And 'stead of supper she would stare
Full hard against the moon. . . ."

Meg Merrilies was so alive to us, it was always a shock to hear the words "God rest her aged bones somewhere! She died full long agone".

This poem was followed by the tragic tale of 'Poor Orphan Joe', who, with 'bare feet blue with cold', trudged through the snow in search of a substitute family. How warm and safe and cosy were we, snuggled in front of the fire, comparing our good fortune with poor Joe's.

". . . A carriage passed by with a lady inside.

She gazed on poor Joe as her own darling child . . ." continued the poem, and of course the lady passed by. His mother was dead, in true Victorian melodrama fashion, and finally a policeman found poor Joe dead on a doorstep. What else!

Mom saved her best till last. We waited with bated breath as she assumed her little girl voice and pose:

"I'm sittin' on the doorstep, an' I'm eatin' bread an' jam.

I ain't a crying, really. Tho' I 'spect ya think I am.

I 'ear the children playin' but they say they don't want me,

Cos my legs are rather likkle, an' I run so slow you see.

So . . . (sigh) I'm sittin' on the doorstep, an' I'm eatin' bread and jam.

I ain't a-cryin' really. Tho' I 'spect ya think I am".

(Sniff . . . sniff).

There was not a dry eye in the house, and the performance was judged a resounding success.

Now it was Margaret's turn to entertain us. She taught us to sing a descant to:

"White coral bells, upon a slender stalk.

Lilies of the Valley deck the garden walk.

Oh, how I wish, that I could hear them ring.

But that can only happen when the fairies sing".

Margaret then recited her favourite poems. This was where I first heard 'Goblin Market', the lovely O'Sullivan poem

"A piper in the street today. Set up a tune and started to play.

And away, away, away on the tide, of his music we

started, on every side.

. . . and little bare feet that were blue with the cold
went dancing back to the age of gold.

And all the world went gay, went gay, for half an
hour, in the street today".

So many lovely impressions and images were stamped
indelibly in the memory during these sessions before the
fire, still dew-fresh after almost forty years. At six-thirty
Mom would take out the large, flat, iron baking plates from
the fireside oven. Clutching them with folded rags she raced
upstairs, to insert in the boys' double bed. They would later
be returned to the oven, to reheat for the girls' beds. If one of
us was really ill there would be the rare treat of a fire in the
bedroom grate.

The boys safely in bed we girls sat on with mom, chatting
companionably or reading. Perhaps there would be 'ITMA'
on the radio, or 'The Goons', both of these shows appealing
to our zany sense of humour.

As the evening wore on an expectant hush settled upon
the cosy gathering, as warm milk for cocoa was heated on
the hob-plate. I always had one ear cocked, listening for the
creak of the garden gate that preceded dad's footfall. He
didn't usually come home until after closing time but there
were exceptions to this rule.

Josy and Margaret didn't fear dad as I did and insisted on
putting the wireless on to get Radio Luxembourg. We had
early discovered the delights of popular music, happily
singing along with the 'pop' idols of the day. But I couldn't
relax now, straining with every fibre of my being to hear the
enemy's approach. With one quick dash I would be through
the hall door and up the stairs, before he even stepped
through the back gate.

Too late. The music had drowned out the 'signal' and dad
was already through the back door and into the living room.
I was trapped, like a petrified rabbit by a stoat. Straight
across the room he strode, imperiously switching off the
radio, before taking his customary seat beside the table. I sat
rigidly with my back to him, staring unseeingly into the
flames.

Wordlessly he held out the 'Express' for mother to take,

as she hovered beside him like a servant waiting on her
master. Next his overcoat was shrugged off into her waiting
hands. She scurried and fawned around him, trying desperately to gauge his mood, her eyes as wild and wide as my
own. He picked up the knife and fork already laid on the
table before him, and mom dashed to the hob's oven where
his dinner was warming. The inverted enamel dinner plate,
placed over the meal in the oven, rattled loudly as she
tremblingly laid dad's meal before him.

'What's this dried up muck?' was the usual retort,
followed by stronger verbal abuse on nights when things
had obviously not gone his way at office or pub. Mom
stood beside him, wringing her hands and chewing her lips,
waiting in dread anticipation. As his vitriolic comments
showered over my mother's bowed head murderous feelings welled up inside me. Yet I did nothing. Said nothing.
Just stared fixedly into the fire. . . waiting to escape.

'Joan'. Father's voice was now velvet-soft. 'My dear
Joan. Come here and take your daddy's shoes off, there's a
good girl'. He thrust his podgy legs out in front of him and
smiled evilly, his dark cold eyes watching my reactions.
Mom leaped forward in a desperate attempt to avert the
charade about to be enacted, kneeling at dad's feet and
beginning to untie his shoe-laces. He timed the gentle
raising of his foot neatly, causing mom to over-balance and
fall at his feet.

'No, mother dear. I said Joan. . . .'

I was powerless to move. Margaret and Josy tried to
intervene, offering good naturedly to take his shoes off if it
made him happy. He ignored them. His plump fingers
began to play with the stout leather belt around what had
once been his waist, then gently, slowly, he undid the brass
buckle. His cold eyes never left my face.

'You are a disobedient child, Joan, and as such must be
punished. Come here'. His barrack-room tones demanded
obedience now, and slowly I crept towards him, intent on
making a sudden dart through the stairs' door behind him,
praying he wouldn't follow me and waken the boys. He was
like a chess player, calculating and computing in advance
the movements of his human pawn. As I broke into a run

the belt shot out, catching me a stinging blow across my bare shins. His evil laugh followed me as I stumbled up the unlit staircase.

Huddled down in my bed I allowed self-pity to engulf me and felt anew the sense of cold, cold loneliness that would be my legacy for years to come. There was no escape, no comfort, no one to turn to. Nobody cared. For hours blessed sleep evaded me. The girls finally came upstairs to their bed across the room from mine, chatting happily, and were soon fast asleep. In the next bedroom I could hear dad's voice droning on and on, telling mother of the day's happenings at the office.

'And I told T.J. I told him he'd lose the contract if he didn't look at the figures again . . . T.J.'s got a lot of respect for my knowledge . . . even tho' he is the Managing Director. . . .'

Again and again I would hear dad get out of bed, hear the unmistakeable sound of him urinating and defecating into the enamel bucket. Finally there would be silence and sleep, and the rude awakening to another wet bed. Then more hours of cold misery until the morning. I tried to make myself think of beautiful flowers and clean countryside, to plan the lovely cottage I would occupy when I grew up, with roses round the door. But I kept coming back to Shelley Road. Sleep brought only nightmares, my father's staring disembodied eyes everywhere.

## CHAPTER NINETEEN

# Father's Poultry Phase.

In the centre of the Willow bed in the new garden we children buried our dead. Birds that the cat had caught and we had tried to revive, always unsuccessfully, their passing accompanied by many tears and a funeral service decently conducted by Margaret. Kneeling beside the tiny grave we would strew flowers over the rag-wrapped body, along with our tears, collectively murmuring the Lord's Prayer as Margaret filled in the soil above the corpse. A stray cat had frozen to death in the lavvy because mom had refused to let it into the house. Soft hearted as she was, she was afraid of disease, and anyway had far too many mouths to feed already. We carried its stiff ginger body tenderly up the garden, and mom gave the man next door ten Woodbines for digging the icy earth to make a grave.

With the onset of dad's Poultry phase we had to perform mass funerals. For three or four weekends in succession he came home on Saturday afternoons with two dozen day-old chicks he had bought from the market. Our joy at their fluffy newness turned to agonised sorrow as their tiny bodies starved to death for want of a broody hen. We walked about with them wrapped in old socks, warmed under our armpits. Still they died. We placed them, wrapped in rags, in the open oven for warmth, but still their delicate eyelids closed forever.

Finally dad had to dig deeper into his pocket and buy a dozen strong pullets, nothing like sweet fluffy chicks. None of us children took to them, but we had no option but to care for them.

Father knocked a crude hole in the rear of the garden shed

and erected a few yards of chicken wire to form a run. Like most such jobs he undertook he skimped on materials and labour, with the inevitable result that the hens were always escaping; Keith and I could regularly be seen running down Shelley Road in hot pursuit of a clucking bird desperate for freedom. Margaret and Josy flatly refused to demean themselves in this manner. We had no option, knowing we would take the blame if a bird went missing.

Mom and us kids now had another daily chore to be coped with. Stale bread was dried in the oven, then mashed into crumbs by folding the bread in a large rag and pounding it with the iron. This was added to the mess of potato peelings mom had to cook in a large saucepan – one of two the family possessed. Its bottom was almost entirely covered with metal washers that dad fitted when it sprang yet another leak. We carried out the mess of peelings, vegetable leaves and bread to the sqawking squabbling birds in the shed. I didn't blame them for being bad-tempered, cooped up as they were in such a confined space. They terrified me with their malevolent looks and threatening beaks, growing daily larger and more vicious.

We were all supposed to clean the Hen House on a roster basis, but the task fell inevitably to Keith and myself. Margaret was not taken in by dad's promise to give mom extra money for Christmas presents for us, when the birds were killed. She darkly and correctly prophesied that the money would only enhance the bank balance of the brewery, and refused to have anything to do with the project. And what Margaret did, Josy did. Once more Keith and I were the labourers, rightly fearing corporal punishment if we neglected our task.

Summer and autumn turned to early winter, and the hens like Topsy before them just 'growed and growed'. Now we just flung their food through the shed window, terrified of the unappealing creatures. Yes, we all hated those fowl–but all agreed that none deserved their ultimate fate.

As Christmas approached we children were told to spread the word amongst our friends that freshly killed birds would be for sale, a few days before Christmas, at eight shillings and sixpence each if I recall correctly. Dad could afford to sell them cheaply – they had only cost him sixpence each, and a few bags of corn. Labour and scraps had been free. It was a bargain and there were plenty of takers.

Once more Margaret tried to negotiate a deal with dad to share the money fairly but he would not be pinned down. She now, at thirteen, held dad in almost total contempt and practically lived at her friend's house two streets away. Their gain was our loss. Josy also made good friends away from Shelley Road and made herself scarce as much as possible. Keith and I were not such taking children and in the winter had nowhere to go but our house.

I did manage to absent myself by babysitting during the whole of Death Day, or 'Bloody Sunday' as it came to be known amongst us Staffords. In the evening I came home to a scene of indescribable carnage, Keith kindly filling me in with the gory details. Our father was a town man-born and bred. The family next door were country people who fished and shot and kept a menagerie of diverse animals over the years, including a monkey. Any one of their sons would have wrung the birds' necks in minutes as an obligement- had dad been anyone else. Instead they watched gleefully from behind the fence as dad struggled to dispatch fowl after slippery fowl.

First he tried the 'broom handle' technique he had heard about. You simply caught your bird, placed its neck under a broom handle, and trod heavily in one quick painless motion. That was the idea, anyway. First dad must catch a bird, a task that would have been easier had he not imbibed so liberally at lunch-time, doubtless filling himself with Dutch Courage for the task ahead. Also, by this time, he was more than stout- he was dreadfully obese. His shape boded no good either in chasing feathered birds nor in leaning down to operate the broom handle.

Puffing and purple with his exertions he finally retired to the kitchen to consult with Keith, who had been hiding in his bedroom watching the performance from behind the curtain, choking with mirth. Dad knew tender-hearted Keith would have no part in the killing, but he had no option but to concede to dad's request for two long pieces of beloved meccano his sons possessed, from the time dad worked briefly for a toy manufacturer. Unwittingly Keith parted with the two lengths and watched with horror as dad constructed a crude tool. With the aid of a few screws he fashioned a long-handled 'guillotine', bolting a fresh razor blade between the shafts. After drinking another couple of pints of beer he was ready.

Keith was sent to catch the birds one at a time, throwing them in the bathroom with dad and closing the door. After an age of scuffling swearing and clucking dad finally emerged, covered from head to foot in feathers, blood and shit. He was closely followed by a bird with its head hanging off, which then proceeded to run obscenely around the kitchen for some time before it finally lay still, legs in the air. Keith promptly took to his heels, gagging and choking, leaving dad to it. For once his troops had totally deserted him and he was forced to do his own dirty work.

When we slunk home that evening there was a row of bloody, almost featherless, dead birds hanging on cup-hooks around the kitchen. The bathroom walls were covered with blood, feathers and muck, the bath part-filled with rapidly congealing blood. Mom had attempted to clean the kitchen but had given up the unequal task and was sitting rocking by the fire. For once we collectively rebelled and refused to clean the bathroom, unable to have baths for days until mom finally gave in. The marks were still on the walls when I papered the bathroom years later.

That night dad rolled home extremely drunk– an unusual occurence for one with so high a tolerance to alcohol. Like Lady Macbeth before him, no matter how he washed his hands the blood must still have clung to them, the scene of slaughter indelibly printed on his mind.

True to Margaret's prophecy we didn't enjoy a single penny of the Hen money. I doubt if dad did– either. Talk about 'blood money'. It is perhaps unnecessary to state that we never kept poultry again.

CHAPTER TWENTY

# Religious Instruction.

We children walked to Sunday School, summer and winter, down Shelley Road, along past the Sewage Farm and railway sidings to the main road. That road must have been over a mile long and seemed endless to us as toddlers, holding fast to Margaret's firm hand. Boredom was alleviated by observing trees, wild flowers and the flowing River Tame. I was fascinated by the long rotating arm sprinkling water over the gravel beds beside the main Sewage works, dragging my feet the better to observe the falling drops of water.

Over the main road and along Keats Street with its posh detached houses and neat suburban gardens. Then the long climb up the hill, along Coleridge Street to our Sunday School in Ridingly. This had been a pretty village when our father grew up there, with rows of quaint cottages and a village green. Now it was shabby, with rows of back-to-back two-up-two-down houses built for the growing industrial developments spilling out from Walsall.

For over a decade we trudged that road past these houses and knew every individual curtain and obligatory front-parlour aspidistra peeping through the sparkling window panes. Pristine doorsteps were either whitened or reddened once weekly to greet the sabbath. Whatever poverty lay behind the primly closed front doors, those houses presented a decently respectable exterior.

Our Sunday School served the local children as an ordinary school during week-days, and had done so for generations. It was a solid Victorian no-nonsense building with towering small-paned sash-windows and solid doors.

I suspect Coleridge Street Sunday School was carefully chosen by our parents because of its distance from Shelley Road, keeping us out of the way and from under mom's feet for the whole of Sunday afternoon. To this day I do not know what denomination it was but suspect, in recalling its evangelical teachings and fervour, that it was Methodist. No Vicar crossed its threshold in all the years we attended, and our Sunday worship was conducted by a Mr. Hodgekiss who wore a sober and decent grey suit. I suppose he must have been a Lay Preacher– he certainly knew his business. A small, squat, typically Staffordshire man with shiny scrubbed countenance, he earned our collective love and respect. Mrs. Hodgekiss was round and motherly, given to wearing flower-strewn hats and pretty voluminous print dresses. She played the piano to accompany our hymns, and loved us all indiscriminately as only some such childless people can.

We gathered together in the main Assembly Hall, sitting on hard wooden benches facing the small wooden stage that Mr. Hodgekiss occupied. The under-fives sat upon the front benches, clucked over by Miss Bacon, a loving hair-pin-thin spinster of uncertain age and great serenity. How I cried when I had to leave her class. Behind the babies sat the older children in separate age-groups, each with a teacher – the oldest children at the rear of the hall. We loved every one of our teachers, prim kindly no-nonsense spinsters with posh voices who smelled of violets or lavender. How dedicated were they in their task of imparting holiness and the scriptures to their poor charges, keeping us in check with gentle admonishments and genteel fingers pressed to pursed lips.

Mr. Hodgekiss led the assembled crowd in prayer and song, and from the earliest age we knew the tunes of the rousing hymns, if not the correct words. I often got the giggles in later years when, now able to read a Hymn Book, I realised what strange words I had hitherto been singing. There were lovely words that rolled off the tongue beautifully, among them the mystical 'Morning has Broken'. Mrs. Hodgekiss thumped out the stirring tunes on the piano and our massed voices yelled in noisy unison.

"Whiter than the Snow..ow..ow..ow. Whiter than the Snow..ow..ow..ow. Wash me in the blood of the Lamb and I shall be whiter than snow". But the picture of myself being washed in blood in our bath at Shelley Road, with a dead lamb lying glassy eyed on the concrete floor, would intrude just when I was trying hardest to be 'holy'. The same with 'Rock of ages, cleft to me. . .' I was told 'cleft' was 'to stick' and I had visions of sticky Rock sticking to me, all old and dirty, and covered in fluff.

After the hymns and prayers, Mr. Hodgekiss told us a heavily-moral tale that usually featured some naughty child who met with a fatal accident before it could repent of its black sins. We were left in no doubt that the poor child was destined to spend Eternity scorched black by Hell-Fire, and week after week I vowed with all my heart I would 'sin no more'. Weekly our preacher made an impassioned plea for us to 'Give Jesus our hands and walk in the ways of the Lord'. Each Sunday I turned over a new leaf, mentally pushing my podgy fist into the ethereal massive hand of God as He reached down from the clouds, fighting Josy when we got home to perform her chores for her and so earn my passage to heaven. Josy would have none of it.

'Joan Mary' she would say primly 'I know you. You're just after something'. Why didn't ANYONE believe I was going to be an angel from now on? By Monday I was back to normal.

I didn't want to go to Hell, certainly, but from an early age I had more than a sneaking suspicion that Heaven wasn't such a good 'cop' either. Our preacher painted a glowing picture of Christ sitting on a golden throne in the middle of a beautifully manicured daisy-strewn field, telling us we could, if good, sit on His right hand in the field. How, I wanted to know, could we ALL sit on his right hand side. We'd stretch all around the world and the last ones would inevitably land up sitting on His left. I was, obviously, a tiresome child and my teachers must have been patience incarnate, but still the doubts persisted.

Again and again, as our teachers patiently told us Bible stories, my mind wandered to the picture of the 'Laughing Cavalier' that graced the plaster-peeling school wall. How supremely handsome he was with his plumed velvet finery, cheeky moustache and insolent laughing eyes. He must have been my first pin-up – even though Margaret nearly spoiled it for me by telling me he had been dead for 'ages'. Looking at a copy of this picture years later I realised with a shock that he bore a striking resemblance to early pictures of my father, and more than resembled my first-love Paul. No doubt some psychiatrist could make a meal of that!

Another lithograph that caught my eye depicted a group of poor Victorian children running, rosy cheeked and laughing, across a wild-flower-strewn meadow. Before I left that Sunday School I knew every detail of that picture, pouring over it with a raptness I rarely gave to my school work. How strange that years later I would discover that the massive oil-painted original was owned by my beloved Leon. He had not suspected it to be of much value, but after hearing I had seen a copy as a child he took it to an art gallery– and sold it for quite a lot of money. Life, I have found, is full of such strange coincidences and portents.

Sunday School, then, is mixed up, as most childhood memories are, with many other extraneous rememberings. I recall how the beams of bright, dusty sunlight fingered the chalky air and lit up the raffia flowers on Mrs. Hodgekiss's straw hat. How that same sunlight shrivelled a Red Admiral butterfly trapped between the open sash window-panes. Before it died it beat its beautiful wings to shreds in a futile attempt to escape its glass prison. Tearfully I begged the teacher to tell someone about its plight– to help it escape to the fresh air outside.

'Joan Mary, be quiet and stop making an exhibition of yourself'.

How could she talk of God caring about every little sparrow that fell–and not lift a finger to help one of God's creatures that He was too busy to attend to? More problems for me to sullenly mull over, born Doubting Thomas that I obviously, sinfully was. How very black I knew was my young soul. I also knew early on that I could not keep one of the Ten Commandments, the one that said 'Honour thy father . . .' Not on your life!.

How old was I when I weighed Christ's suffering upon

the Cross–and knew it was as nothing compared to the agonies children suffer at the hands of cruel adults– their pain lasting a lifetime-their suffering unwitnessed by loving Disciples. He chose His Calvary, I reasoned, while such children had no option.

Each Sunday we were given a beautifully illustrated Text to learn for the following week. No pressure was put upon us or reward offered, yet we committed those texts to memory just to please our teachers. "Behold I stand at the door and knock . . ." (Poor Jesus, bravely bearing that bloody crown of thorns as he patiently knocked on the ivy-sealed door of my heart. But what was to stop Him putting his lamp down and removing the nasty crown?) Isaiah 55, Verses six and seven, "Seek ye the Lord where He may be found . . ." is indelibly printed on my mind, along with hundreds of other verses from the Bible. How often, in my many agnostic 'Dark Nights of the Soul', I have found comfort in those well-remembered words.

Most fascinating and repelling of all were the Magic Lantern Shows. Enlarged black and white photographs of unfortunate lepers were projected onto a hung sheet-screen. Black piccaninnies looked out sorrowfully from the screen, bravely bearing their mutilated limbs for all to see. Stumps of fists with fingers eaten away, toes missing and blind-socket eyes. Sick and shaken I raced home to beg for 'Pennies for the Lepers' . . . but to no avail. What price lepers when mom and neighbours could barely feed, clothe or warm their children? I early felt angry, sorry and impotent to help suffering, while at the same time counting my blessings. For days after these shows I carefully inspected my arms and legs for the telltale white patches that would herald the onset of leprosy. No one had told me it wasn't rife in the West and I had visions of trying to write at school clutching a pencil in my fingerless fist. Another nightmare to add to the growing store. Perhaps people were right when they said I had too much imagination for my own good and 'always got 'old of the wrong end of the stick'.

All of us children grew to love Coleridge Street Sunday School, its preacher and teachers, and were regularly presented with religious Book Prizes denoting 'First Prize for Attendance'. It was a stable secure part of my young life, giving me much spiritual comfort until I lost my faith at the age of about eleven. Gradually I had awakened to the fact that I could not believe in a 'loving God' who allowed my mother to suffer so, and dad to go unpunished.

From then on Keith and I regularly played truant, amusing ourselves and annoying the residents of Coleridge Street by 'paling hopping' over the back fences of their gardens and running away before they could catch us, or knocking on their doors then dashing away to hide.

Sunday School gave us a good grounding in Bible Study and left us with a legacy of beautiful hymns. In adulthood I learned, without surprise, that Christina Rossetti helped to write the words of 'In the Bleak Midwinter . . .' and Eleanor Farjeon was responsible for the beautiful words of 'Morning has Broken . . .' Both of these women had long been favourite poets. Coleridge Street provided a sweet, kindly contrast to Shelley Road and I'm sure we all benefited from our years of enforced attendance. Yet of the five of us children only Margaret remained religious. The rest of us grew up to be 'God-fearing atheists'. The seeds of my spirituality were, however, well sown finally germinating in middle age.

## CHAPTER TWENTY-ONE

# Some Neighbours.

On the opposite corner to our house in Shelley Road lived the Jones family. Father considered all of our neighbours to be of a lower class than ourselves, and while we did not necessarily share his view we had to admit that the Jones's abode was indisputedly a slum.

Mrs. Jones spent most of the day balancing her colossal bosom upon what was left of the garden gate. From this vantage point she could keep an eye on her numerous off-spring, whilst enjoying a 'cant' with various neighbours as they scurried to and from the shops or bus-stop. Small, almost as round as she was high, she was still a handsome woman with masses of black greasy ringlets and dark gypsy eyes.

Her husband, a large silent man, adored her and their children. When his war wound permitted he worked as a stoker in the local Steel Foundry, handing his pay-packet unopened to his wife. He was always busy, scurrying about collecting bits of coal that fell onto the railway siding, or raking through rubbish tips in search of old mattresses and bedsteads, broken chairs and old saucepans. These gifts he bore home in triumph to 'Mother', like a bird bringing his mate scraps for their nest.

The youngest of their children was Sammy. He was 'delicate', given to taking fits, and walked with a limp. Mrs. Jones seemed inordinately proud of these afflictions, never tiring of regaling passers-by with details of the origin of Sammy's ills.

"E wuz stuck fast, see, an' 'is likkle leg cum fairst and the nairse couldn't shift 'im. Only babby wot I 'ad trouble wiv.

Hours an' hours 'e wuz stuck 'till the nairse run an' fetched the Docta. 'E 'ad to gerr 'im out wiv them forceps things. Dain't breathe for ages . . . poor likkle sod'. Sammy, basking in the reflected glory of his birth, played happily in the gutter under his mother's fond gaze.

There were numerous big brothers who disappeared from time to time, escorted by the local bobby, returning at intervals with closely cropped hair and smart Reformatory clothes. Later, when these boys became eligible for National Service, the Military Police were regular visitors to Shelley Road.

Keith and I only once went into their house, looking for the correct change for our electricity meter. We usually went to the bus terminus a few streets away, so it was probably just an excuse to see inside the Jones's house. I began to gag with the stench whilst still on the front doorstep. Keith, enjoying being the tough man, grinned amicably at Mrs. Jones and said we'd be delighted to step into the parlour. Much as I loved my brother, I had to admit he did have more than a touch of father's sadism.

Inside the living room all internal doors and fixed cupboards had been roughly removed, probably for fire-wood. A large blazing fire, a rare sight for us, roared in the filthy, never-black-leaded grate. The floorboards felt tacky underfoot and I didn't dare look down and examine this phenomenon more closely. On the shapeless torn sofa two lurchers took their ease, surrounded by sundry yapping, grunting, guzzling pups.

The table in the centre of the room was covered with old newspapers on which reposed a large loaf, breadknife, margarine in its wrapper and a sticky jar of jam. Mrs. Jones' toffee pan, the main tool of her occasional trade as a maker and purveyor of Toffee Apples, also littered the table. From this pan a large malevolent-looking black cat licked, inter-rupted now and then by numerous grubby fingers dipping in. Mom had always refused our requests for a penny to buy a Jones's toffee apple and now we knew why.

The residue on the floorboards was explained when Sammy wandered in grinning vacantly, squatting down in the middle of the floor with a contented sigh and embarrassing sounds. I dashed for the back door, trying not to breathe and saying 'Thank you, Mrs Jones' at the same time.

The garden, from where the Jones' boys ran their scrap empire, was almost as bad as the house, making Steptoe's Yard look like something out of the 'Ideal Home' Magazine. And yet, I later reflected when I had recovered my breath if not my lunch, that family was to be envied. There was a tangible warmth about them, a basic caring for each other that many families lacked. They would all have defended each other to the death and spoke to each other with a kindly consideration. They were a true family unit, vibrant and strong, destined to survive long after families such as ours had fallen apart.

Living next door to the Jones's were the O'Sheas, an elderly couple who shared their home with one slightly simple batchelor son. They had one older son who had spent the War with the Eighth Army in the East. After the Armistice a street party was arranged to welcome home our local hero. Strands of gay bunting were draped around the houses, and Union Jacks fluttered from upstairs windows. 'Welcome Home, Billy Boy', shouted a roughly-painted placard above O'Shea's front door. On the morning of Billy's expected arrival a telegram arrived, announcing that Billy had been killed in an accident on the way home. The old couple died shortly afterwards. They just faded tearfully away leaving their simple son to fend for himself.

The next house was occupied by the Murphys. Mr. Murphy had been an Air-Raid Warden and had been killed 'doing his duty'. His widow was a tiny frail bird-like creature who took to her bed in the living room shortly after the war. Keith and I dreaded her tap tapping on the window pane, summoning us to run an errand for her. We would hastily avert our eyes and talk in loud animated voices, as we strolled by. Sometimes she struggled to the front door in her nightgown and conscience got the better of us.

She had three grown-up sons and one daughter. The eldest son, Charlie, was a big brute of a man, an iron-fisted bachelor miner with an addiction to strong drink. He terrorised his weaker brothers and sister, and it was rumoured that he had once attacked his mother with a poker. Brian, the second eldest Murphys' son, was a tall gentle, aesthetic-looking handsome man with a 'wracking' cough. He faded away in his mid-twenties from tuberculosis. The youngest brother was frail and rather vacant. It was he that our gentle Margaret, his contemporary, hit over the head with a shovel for kicking our dog.

The daughter of the family was Betty, still unmarried in her mid-twenties. A plain girl with carroty hair she had a menial job in a local factory and was not of the highest intellect. Margaret, ever wishing to make silk purses out of sows' ears, so to speak, persuaded Betty to allow herself to be made up and have her hair crimped with mom's curling tongs. At sixteen Margaret already had the makings of the light novelist she has studied to become, and was always endeavouring to organise people's lives into happy endings.

Betty was smuggled into our house behind dad's back and Margaret skilfully applied foundation, rouge and eyeshadow. Betty even submitted herself to the torture of having her shaggy eyebrows plucked. From her own meagre 'wardrobe' Margaret selected a few choice items to complete the transformation.

Not wishing to waste her handiwork Margaret persuaded her protégé to go, that evening, to the cinema and I was deputed to accompany her as a chaperone. We took the bus into Walsall and made our way to the Palace, commonly known as the 'Scabby Alice', unarguably the seediest cinema for miles around. A war film entitled 'They were not Divided' was being shown. I saw it, Betty didn't.

A few minutes after we had taken our seats a man with long black brilliantined hair asked Betty if she minded him sitting beside her. She simpered her consent and I was handed a few sweets and told to sit a few rows in front. Only weeks later they were married and I was a bridesmaid.

Margaret, viewing things as usual through rose-tinted spectacles, said it was a Fairy Tale Romance. I stubbornly persisted in my belief that Betty had got her man under false pretences, and no good would come of it. They lived unhappily ever after. Some Fairy tale!

## CHAPTER TWENTY-TWO

# Signs of Womanhood.

I was in no hurry to grow up and endure periods, being both revolted and distressed by the thought of blood pouring from my bottom. Not that periods were talked about much. I had gleaned my little knowledge from overheard whispered conversations at home, and from the crude grape-vine of the school playground. The bloody rags soaking in a bucket in the bathroom, plus the one talk on hygiene when I started Technical College, almost prepared me.

'Hands up those who are going swimming this week' requested Miss Holcroft.

'Please Miss, me Miss'. My hand was happily waved each week, all the pupils looking pityingly at those girls who sat in embarrassed silence, their hands in their laps. Thankfully there were no boys in class, although the school was nominally co-educational. We joined the boys only for dancing, singing and the Christmas party.

I knew, anyway, which girls were menstruating at a particular time. A heavy, fishy smell hung about them like an evil cloud, nauseating and repelling.

'Ain't yow started yet? Must be som 'at wrong wi' ya. Yow won't be able to 'ave babbies, ya know'. I didn't care, not one bit. Yuk!

One morning, when I was about fourteen and a half, I awoke to strange whirrings inside my tummy. Not pain, but a sensation of cogs and wheels of delicate machinery gathering momentum. Feeling flushed and faintly light-headed I lay listening apprehensively to my body, trying to understand the strange phenomena.

'Come on, Jo. You'll be late for school. You're dawdling again'. Margaret was already half dressed, having to be out earlier than me to get to her job at the library. She despaired of my tardy ways. Moving to sit up I felt the warm flow running from me. I had stopped wetting the bed at eleven or twelve but was still wary of a recurrence. I shot quickly out of bed; bright blood ran down my legs. Somewhere inside my head I screamed 'No. No . . . No'.

Margaret ran downstairs and quickly reappeared with a clean rag which she expertly folded into a tube, showing me how to pin it with two nappy pins to my vest. I felt sick and betrayed. Another secret to keep from Keith. Another nail in the coffin of childhood.

Walking leaden-footed down Shelley Road to catch the school bus I pondered on many things. Margaret had told me that this would happen once a month until I was forty. Twelve times twenty-five made . . . No, I couldn't manage that sum, but I did know it added up to a mind-boggling figure. My life stretched out before me like a prison sentence, with no reprieve. And if a man so much as embraced me and kissed me passionately I could have a baby. I had yearned to be loved and kissed by some nice kind person ever since I could remember. Now even that was out of the question.

Waiting for the bus at the main road I recall realising, for the first time, that I was 'under-privileged'. Snow was lying dirtily underfoot and staining the toes of my white ankle-socks. My only footwear was a pair of brown sandals with the toes cut out. I had grown taller than my sisters and my feet were consequently larger so I could no longer inherit their cast-offs. My bunions, caused by wearing too-narrow shoes on my broad feet, ached with the cold. Each morning I traced around the soles of the sandals with a pencil and cut out an inner-sole from a Corn Flakes box, to cover the holes in my sandals. The cardboard was already wet and soggy, chilblains itching to distraction.

Since early childhood my legs had ached in the mornings sometimes so badly that I had to shuffle downstairs on my bottom. Mum said it was growing pains. The pain would lessen during the day, often disappearing entirely until next morning. I think it was a form of rheumatics from lying in wet beds. Now my bare legs hurt to the bone, the cold wind searching out each aching sinew. The thin school skirt chafed my knees and I was embarrasingly aware that it was too short for me. Vest, school shirt and blazer protected my upper limbs. No scarf or gloves. No top-coat. At my feet my school satchel, Margaret's old one, was roughly cobbled here and there with frayed string. The handle was missing entirely, replaced by a piece of rope.

The wooden slats of the bus seat dug deep into my body and jolted my spine. The icy blast from the open platform fingered the core of my being. The lumpy rag between my legs felt alien. Would I ever be warm again? Run free again?

In class there was the ever-present fear of blood seeping through my skirt, and when passing boys in the corridors I felt the lumpy rag and pins must be protruding for all to see. During the course of the day I grew more and more distressed, as the rag began to smell. For a child who was fastidious about body smells it was a nightmare.

After school, walking with a few friends to the bus stop, I caught sight of my dad. He was waiting to cross the road and we would have to pass close to him. I knew he would ignore me and that I must not acknowledge him in public. He had told me repeatedly he had only two daughters, Margaret and Josy. Smart and military, he carried his small rotund figure proudly. Wavy hair neatly combed, pipe clenched between teeth and sensual lips, double chins straining at his snow-white shirt and Regimental tie, he strode past me, almost touching me with his furled umbrella. His cold eyes met mine for a brief second, without a flicker of recognition.

I looked back and watched him striding purposefully towards Green Lane and the seedier quarters of Walsall. One of my school friends, who lived in that direction, had previously told me of seeing father, with a woman, coming out of a house there.

'Hey, Jo', my best friend Anne nudged me in the ribs. 'Dain't ya see yer dad? 'E just went past'. Immediately some merry quip sprang to my lips and I was all laughter and light-heart, playing like mad to the gallery.

Alone, on the bus bearing me back home, acute misery once more held me in chains. The soiled rag chaffed my legs. The hard pin dug into my spine. The two mile journey seemed endless.

For some weeks I had noticed a very tall blond school boy, a man almost, who entered the bus at the stop I alighted from. He was like a young god, remote from my world, clean and smart, with a beautiful posh accent. Sometimes, if I was dreaming and forgot my stop until the last moment, I had to squeeze past him in the gang-way of the bus, thrilling at the contact of his warm body so close to mine. When this happened my legs felt wobbly, and I experienced a strange sensation of intense pleasure deep inside my lower tummy. Simultaneously hot blood rushed to my cheeks betraying my confusion, as I rushed past him with lowered eyes. Today I was careful to be on the platform, ready to alight at my stop, in case he should feel the lump in my skirt, or smell me. I remembered the Black Death and thought perhaps I should have a hand-bell to ring shouting 'Unclean' as I passed through the streets. Even this thought failed to amuse me.

At the bus stop near the shops were gigantic hoardings. From one of them, advertising Lux toilet soap, the current darling of the silver screen smiled provocatively down at passing strangers. I stood for a moment admiring the beautiful Veronica Lake of the peek-a-boo hairstyle, her softly blonde shining hair almost obscuring one eye. She looked so clean and wholesome and I knew that I belonged in her world, not Shelley Road. 'It ain't fair, It ain't fair', I yelled silently to myself as I trudged towards our house.

Mum was sitting by the fire, bare blotchy legs a mass of scabs that never healed, her fingers always nervously scratching and scrawping at her shins. She always wore a faded print dress with spots on that I had christened her 'aspirin' frock when I was a little girl.

'How've you been, mum?'.

'A'right, I 'spect'. Dull eyes searched my face, then lit up as she remembered her motherly duties. She reached behind her to the built-in cupboards and conspiratorially handed me a clean rag.

''Ere. You'll need a clean 'un. Put th' other one in the bucket'.

'Can I have a bath, mum? Is the water hot enough?' Her eyes opened wide in horror and alarm.

'Ya can't 'ave a bath when you'm like that' she said, inclining her head in the general direction of my stomach.

'Why can't I?' A bath I certainly needed and was determined to have. She screwed up her face in child-like concentration, chewing slowly on her single tooth, gathering her thoughts.

'It meks ya weak. An' ya mustn't wash yer 'air, neither, till you've finished yer you-know-whats. Ya can get blood ta the brain. No sittin' on cold doorsteps an' things, neither. That's very dangerous'. Exhausted by this unusually long conversation she sank back into her chair and her own world. I went into the kitchen and cut myself a slice of bread. Mum didn't bother much with cooking now. In fact she didn't bother much with anything. Sometimes, after there had been real ructions between dad and the family, I was afraid to come home in case she'd carried out her threat and put her head in the gas oven.

Margaret would be in from work at six o'clock, so I prepared something for her to eat and organised the boys' tea. Sometimes, still, mum made super-human efforts to run the household but generally she sat by the fire, crying silently and rocking to and fro. The Babby, nearly ten years old did most of the week-day shopping and firelighting. Keith, at twelve and a half, helped with a milk round before school and a paper round afterwards, handing most of his earnings over to mom. Dad reduced her allowance accordingly.

Josy and Margaret came in from work together, catching the same bus from Walsall. They wore discreet make-up, curled their hair fashionably, and both had serious boyfriends. After tea I told Margaret what mum had said about bathing and hair washing. Since starting work Margaret spoke 'nicely' and I was trying hard to copy her. She spoke authoritatively.

'Take no notice, Jo. Mum's old-fashioned, and anyway that's just Old Wives' Tales. You have a bath if you wish'.

Margaret knew I usually did what I wanted, being the most rebellious and headstrong child in the family.

I escaped into the bathroom and locked the door. I ran a deep bath and thankfully removed the soiled rag, dunking it into the bucket with the snot-rags which were always soaking in salt water. Soon I was sweet and clean again, hair washed in Persil soap-powder in the absence of shampoo, which only posh people could afford. Margaret sometimes treated herself to one, mixing the white powdered shampoo carefully with cold water. It took ages to get rid of the lumps.

Standing on the concrete floor before the flyblown, spotted, cracked mirror wedged drunkenly above the wash-hand basin, I began to comb my shoulder-length hair dry. I hadn't bothered much with my appearance prior to this day, but suddenly I felt a rush of excitement, seeing my hair fall into a natural wave over my right eye just like Veronica Lake's. Posing before the mirror I realised, for the first time, that I was quite pretty in a strange sort of way. It was unbelievable.

I fished out Margaret's make-up bag from under the sink and unskilfully applied black eye-brow pencil to eye-brows, and right around my eyes. Mascara-brush was spat upon, as I had seen my sisters do, and applied haphazardly to eyelashes. I regretted for the millionth time that I did not possess Josy's thick eyelashes, nor her eyes which were of a much deeper blue than mine. Hastily I applied a touch of lipstick to my cheeks and rubbed it below the high fine cheek-bones. Full lips were soon drawn into a scarlet cupid's bow.

Wielding Margaret's precious toothbrush I scrubbed my teeth with her Gibbs toothpaste, a solid pink cake in a round tin. On close examination the teeth were not over-large, as I had thought. It was a pity about the gap, but it had narrowed and was not VERY ugly. Ponds Cold Cream was massaged into neck and hands, 'Midnight in Paris' splashed liberally on wrists and behind ears.

Piling baby-fine mass of fair hair on top of my head with both hands, I posed before the mirror, revelling now in my budding breasts, tiny waist, and swelling hips. Peering down at my legs I gloried in the fact that the extra four inches of height I had over my sisters, was all added to my legs. I was the only one in proportion. It all went to my head and I felt powerful, strong and seductive. Beguiled by my own beauty I decked myself in imaginary finery, transporting myself to a flowery bower. My boy-off-the-bus knelt at my feet, begging for my hand. It could not be. I was promised to another . . . Tears clouded my eyes at the sadness of eternal parting . . .

'Jo, are you going to be in there all day? I've got to go out in a minute and I've not done my face yet. Come on . . .'.

Hastily I replaced my sister's make-up and scrubbed my face with the face rag. On with vest and hated school clothes. A last glance in the mirror at the new hair style, softly falling over one eye. I tossed my hair back as I had seen other 'big' girls do, temporarily clearing my vision. From now on a comb would be a vital part of my school uniform. From the mirror my startled wide eyes stared back at me, puzzled. Who was I? Then I remembered the rag and pins I must again wear, and shuddered . . . I was just plain Jo, period. Ugh!

As I walked through to the living room to do my homework, I was shocked to see dad sitting at the table. Oh, no! What had he come home for? He usually went straight from work to the pub. He was a ghastly purple colour and his eyes bulged glassily as he fought for breath, having recently been diagnosed asthmatic. I slunk into the corner of the room and tried to concentrate on my homework. Dad's eyes bored into me. I read my book. He stared . . . and stared . . . he was quite capable of doing it for hours, knowing I'd finally break and start to scream. Eventually he spoke between gasps.

'What have you done to your hair, girl. You look as if you're hiding under a bloody tree'. He laughed wheezily at his own wit. Still I did not look up, although tears had started at the back of my eyes.

'I have found a new nick-name for you, Joan. It is 'Mildew'. A green slime found lying up against walls . . . Do you like it?'

His earlier nick-names for me had included 'Four-Eyes',

'Horse-Chops', 'Paling Teeth' and 'Pinty' which was short for pin-toed; all these names being keyed to my more obvious physical defects. I tried hard to think what had prompted 'Mildew'. Yes, I had it! Last week Josy had asked me to make up a foursome with herself, her boyfriend and his brother. We had gone to the cinema to see a musical. The boys had escorted us back to Shelley Road and I had been left talking at the gate to 'my' spotty, dull youth, while Josy and her boyfriend 'snogged' round the corner. Dad had come home early from the pub and seen me.

Father's voice was full of innuendo as he delivered his parting shot to my retreating figure.

'Yes, Joan. You are right to take a bath so often'.

From that day forward he called me a prostitute, and told me the sooner I left home to live on my earnings the better.

CHAPTER TWENTY-THREE

# Last Year of Schooling.

Queen Elizabeth the Second had just been crowned Queen of England. It was a joyous year, with street parties and celebrations everywhere. These continued throughout the rest of Nineteen Fifty-Three, and our Technical College hired a ballroom and band to mark the occasion. After the hardship of the war years the world erupted in gaiety and colour, and we were lucky to be part of that era.

We only mixed with the boys at our College for singing lessons. They were, therefore, simply remote figures that brushed against us occasionally in the corridors. Now we had to learn to dance with them.

Our dancing teacher, Mrs. Williams, was a short dumpy body, very Welsh, bossy and strident. In the few short months before the College Dance she drilled us unmercifully, until we were all proficient in the execution of the Foxtrot, Waltz, Quickstep, Tango and Rhumba. We were also taught the rudiments of Highland Dancing.

Our first lesson was terrifying. Boys were lined up on one side of the Assembly Hall, girls on the other. Mrs. Williams explained to the boys the courtesies of inviting a lady to partner them, addressing herself to forty adolescent and mainly callow youths and girls. On went the record player, the strains of the 'Blue Danube' filled the dusty air, and the boys were instructed to advance towards us. Back pressed up against the wall I waited, with inward terror and apprehension. One of the Prefects was ambling purposefully towards me.

'Excuse me, Joan, may I have the pleasure of this dance?'
On the dance floor his arm encircled my waist tightly; I

felt like a bird caught in a snare. He was very tall, my eyes just came level with the top button of his blazer. Mrs. Williams' shrill voice echoed down the hall.

'Joan Stafford. Will you please allow Robert to hold your hand. He's not going to bite you. Off you go. . .One. . . Two. . .Three. One. . .' I felt the eyes of the other pupils upon us and heard their subdued giggling. Robert and I began to dance, inexpertly at first, but soon our young bodies moved in unison.

Robert was the tallest, most handsome, boy in the College. He was also the oldest, at almost sixteen, with a wispy shadowy moustache and sleeked-back, lightly brilliantined hair. He lived in a big house on Lichfield Street, and I knew his father was a doctor. A lot of the girls in my class had a 'pash' for Robert; girls with shining curls and nice clothes. Finally Anne, my best friend, told me why Robert fancied me. 'Me big bruther told me th' other day, after we met 'im an' 'is pal in the park. Remember? When you an' me was wiv your Josy? Well, I dain't like to tell you in case you was offended. Our Billy said your Josy was the beautifullest gairl 'e'd ever sin, but you was the sexy-lookin' one'. I tried to imagine what sexy looking meant as applied to myself. I wasn't at all sure it was what I wanted. I deliberately walked hunched-shouldered to conceal my budding breasts, while most of the girls in my class proudly displayed theirs.

Robert had been a Boy Soprano and even though his voice had broken he still practised in the college hall, under Mrs. Williams' tutelage. Sitting at my desk on the floor above the hall I could hear him clearly, his voice soaring out of the open casement windows and on up into the sulphurous haze that hung perpetually over Walsall.

"Oh, for the wings, for the wings of a dove.. Far, far away, far away would I roam. . . ." The music and words stirred something deep inside me, releasing my spirit to soar unfettered for a few brief moments.

Mrs. Williams had only joined the staff in this my final year of schooling, hastily forming us into a choir and selecting solo singers for the Coronation Concert. Her taste was catholic and cultured. From her we learned 'Linden

Lea', The Welsh National Anthem in both Welsh and English, 'Annie Laurie', 'Who is Sylvia', and the beautiful "I leave my heart in an English garden. Safe where the roses of England grow. . . ." Singing this song, I first became aware of my own 'Englishness', loving, as I did, the leafy lanes, canals and patches of woodland that still surrounded the sprawling industrial estates around Walsall. I have never since heard this song, but recall the words and tune effortlessly, together with the glorious emotions I experienced when I sang them:

"Breezes in the long grass ruffling my hair.
Hollyhock and Bluebell scenting the air.
Nothing in the world could ever be
Such a sweet . . . melody.
Nothing in the world was ever so fair."

Mrs. Williams also taught us the stirring 'Men of Harlech', the gentle 'Morning has Broken' and 'My love is like a Red, red rose. . . .' In a few short months we were word perfect for the next Concert.

This teacher was gifted with enthusiasm, and we responded to her, despite her strictness. She, alone, imparted to me the few elements of real culture I acquired during ten years of full-time education. We were taught nothing of other Languages, Poetry, the Classics or Shakespeare, although we did spend one whole lesson drawing Anne Hathaway's Cottage during a History lesson.

Margaret inadvertently opened up the world of poetry for me at about this time. From the library where she worked she brought home 'Palgrave's Golden Treasury'. In this I found Thomas Hood's, "I Remember, I remember, the house where I was born. . ."; a poem she had taught us in childhood, always my favourite. Entranced, I carried on to read 'Palgrave' from cover to cover, swallowing Shelley, Keats and Byron in one great gulp. I still recall the feeling of sheer delight on discovering Shelley's "The fountains mingle with the river, and the river with the ocean. . . ." My awakening senses thrilled to the certain knowledge that the crude sexual couplings, glimpsed both at home and along alleys and fields around Shelley Road, were not what sex was all about.

Margaret began to bring home biographies of poets, and looking back I see that this was where my literary education began. Never again would I be totally imprisoned in Shelley Road. Now I could walk freely with Shelley at sunset; meet with the rascally Byron, or sit an hour with the gentle Keats.

I wrote a poem myself, labouring all one evening over a sweet verse about Alpine flowers in springtime. Margaret praised the poem and sent it off as a contribution to a Poetry Magazine her old school was publishing. Twenty years later Margaret told me that the Editor, Margaret's old English master, refused to believe a child of fourteen had written the poem, rejecting it on those grounds. I do wish she had told me earlier.

Our Christmas Dance at the College was a huge success but marred, for me, by my shyness and lack of finery. Mum was nagged into buying me a cheap New-Look–length circular skirt in flame coloured taffeta, for an early Christmas present. The skirt might have been a success had I not had to wear my school shirt and cardigan, ankle socks and plimsolls. The other girls, every single one of them, wore proper party dresses, court shoes and lisle stockings.

I shrank away into a corner and refused to dance with Robert, burning with embarrassment and anger. Anger at dad for spending all the money on booze, anger at mum for not standing up to him. Anger at God. Anger at injustice. Half-way through the Dance I made my escape and trudged home wearily through the dark streets. The two mile journey to our house seemed endless. Mum hadn't even been able to afford the two pennies for bus fare. Christmastime, 1953. Not even Shelley could have warmed me that night.

In two months time I would be fifteen and could legally leave school at Easter. I played truant a lot of the time until then. I didn't care. I had no shoes or even sandals, and I was so very ashamed of wearing 'pumps' in winter. I couldn't wait to leave school and start earning some money.

CHAPTER TWENTY-FOUR

# Fifteenth Birthday.

It was a bitterly cold February morning in Nineteen Fifty-Four, my fifteenth birthday. In the early hours of the morning I had had one of my frequent nightmares, my body convulsing so violently that the bed had collapsed. This often happened as there was a nut missing from a crucial bolt holding the top left hand corners of the iron-framed bed together.

The combined shock of nightmare and collapsing bed were almost too much for me, causing my hands to tremble like those of a palsied old lady as I reassembled the heavy bed, feet aching with cold on the bare floor boards. Clothed only in an outgrown, washed-thin nightie and old cardigan, I grappled with the horsehair mattress and paper-thin torn sheets. It didn't take long to make the bed, just one doubled army blanket and dad's old army greatcoat.

Snuggled down under the covers I surveyed the bedroom, eerily shadowed in the early morning light. The ceiling was a criss-cross of cracked plaster and grey stains from the cold water tank in the eaves. One of our childish bedtime games had been to make out pictures and fantastic shapes among the cracks, much as one can 'see' pictures in a fire.

Across the room I could dimly make out the shape of the double bed where my sisters slept, cosily cuddled together for warmth. The winter winds searched the empty fire-place, sighing sadly of something loved and lost. The walls were bare of pictures and the emulsioned green walls, painted by the Council in 1937 when the house was built, were a mess of scabbed peeling plaster. The skimpy curtains, faded and threadbare, made a vain attempt to stretch across the long window, sagging in the centre on slack string. The street lamp on the corner of Shelley Road suffused the small window-panes with soft golden light, gilding the fern-frost patterning the inside of the glass.

Goods trains shunted and squealed a few hundred yards away, at the railway junction behind the house. Born to that sound, it was comforting and familiar. Lying in my usual foetal position, meditating deeply, I strove to find some meaning to life. Who was I? Why was I here? In this house? In this family? For what purpose had I been born? God had been lost to me for some years, along with Santa Claus, Saints and Innocence. I simply refused to believe in a 'loving' God who allowed myself and my mother to suffer so, both as a child and an adult.

For all of my life I had ached for human embrace, searching for love as a parched man would search for water in a desert. My second birthday had brought Keith, and later there had been the Babby, and mum had reserved her maternal love for the boys. Dad took the rest of her love, and she loved him with total surrender, pecking greedily at the tiny crumbs of caring he scattered at her famished board. These were facts long since accepted.

Who, I wondered, would bother about my birthday? Margaret would have bought a card, and had it signed by my siblings. There would also be a small, thoughtfully chosen present. Last year, the year she started work, she had given me a fountain pen. It was my most treasured possession. My Godmother next door, banned from visiting the house, would watch for me in the street and slip me a shilling.

'Don't tell ya dad, Joan Mary. What the eye don't see. . . .'

My babies were too young to know about birthdays. Since the age of eleven years I had earned my pocket-money by looking after neighbours' babies. At fifteen I was an old hand at bathing, changing, burping, pacifying, feeding and rocking them to sleep. I clung to their soft warm bodies with a desperate need, deeply humbled by their dependence upon me. Mothers from streets around knew to send for me if they had a sick or mardy baby, sending coded messages through Keith when dad was in residence. No one called at our house openly. No friends or neighbours. We had long since devised a sort of morse code to signal to our friends, as we sought to outwit the enemy. At fifteen I was skilled in cunning and infinitely street-wise.

Dad rarely used the belt on me now, contenting himself with pushing me 'accidentally' out of his way, so that I fell, usually against a wall. He was a master of sadistic, verbal abuse. Mum, in a rare moment of lucidity, said to me one day.

''E says such terrible things ta me. I'd rather 'e gid me a black eye. It wouldn't 'urt so much'.

These thoughts led me on to murder, a subject that Keith and I had been discussing for some time. Dad's murder to be exact. Probably by stabbing with his own knife, the one that he used for carving the miniscule Sunday joint. The sound of a knife being honed still sickens me, and must be performed out of ear-shot. This knife had a special place in the kitchen, safely out of the reach of young fingers. We knew how lethal it was because, some months before, Keith had used it to cut some string I was holding. The knife sliced painlessly half-way through my thumb, severing an artery. Yes, it was certainly fit for the job of disposing of father.

Outside the bedroom window I heard a rattle of milk bottles as the milk-cart stopped to let Keith off. He was back from his rounds and would be frozen. I dashed downstairs and put the kettle on the stove. A few minutes later a small fire was going and Keith knelt before the flames, spreading purple swollen fingers before him. He had no overcoat and had been up since 4 a.m. delivering milk, in a vain attempt to help mum to make ends meet. But since Margaret and Josy started work dad had cut down mum's allowance even further. He gave her four pounds a week, out of which she paid all household bills. She even had to pay the Hire Purchase on dad's own clothes because she was terrified of debt collectors. Dad never paid any bills.

Keith was tiny and bird-like, daintily handsome. His blond hair was greased with margarine and coaxed to a point at the back in the fashionable Tony Curtis D.A. He knelt before the fire, head bowed to hide the tears that ran down his pinched cheeks as his hands came painfully back to life. For the rest of his life he would never be able to fully straighten his fingers, nor rid his left arm of the marks from dad's persistent precisely-aimed punches.

'Jo. Ya know what I 'eard 'im say to our mom yesterday? 'E said 'er was 'avin' it off with me while 'is back was turned. The dirty bastard. 'E's fuckin' sick. 'Ave ya thought any more about doin' 'im in? Stabbin' 'im in the gut's too clean for 'im, really'.

Kind soft hearted Keith, sensitive and caring about all animals, I knew he could have killed dad without a second's thought. So could I have done. It wouldn't have bothered us any more than cracking one of our dog's fleas.

We discussed which one of us should do it. Should we toss a coin? And, as murder was still a hanging offence, we would have to dispose of the body. Everyone, we agreed, would believe he had just gone off with one of his women. If we were discovered we would plead self-defence, reckoning there might be enough people to stand up in court and vouch for our dad's cruelty to us.

Clutching cups of steaming tea we whispered our plans, giving vent to our hurt and hatred. It helped us both, gave us hope of freedom from our torturer. We fell silent as Margaret came downstairs and went through to the kitchen. Keith reached across and touched my hand, his mouth twisted into a lop-sided, bitter grin.

'Naw. Jo. We'll never do it, will we? 'E ain't werth it. Cum on, smile. 'Appy Berthday'. He reached into his pocket and handed me a Mars Bar.

''Ere our kid, get stuck inta that'.

*Joan Mary aged two*

*Joan Mary aged seven*

*Jo Mary (Joanne) aged seventeen*

## WALSALL EDUCATION COMMITTEE

### WALSALL TECHNICAL COLLEGE
#### SECONDARY DEPARTMENT

# REPORT

PRINCIPAL
E. JEWITT, B.Sc. (Eng.) A.I.E.E.
TELEPHONE No. 1124

Secondary ................ Dec. ........ Spring ........ Term, 1953 ........ 1st. ........ Year

NAME ... Joan.

Position in Class ........ Number in Class 24

| SUBJECT | Homework % | Class or Lab. Work % | Exam. % | REMARKS | Initials of Lecturer |
|---|---|---|---|---|---|
| English | 60 | 68 | 67 | That she is capable of much better work | |
| History | 65 | 60 | 61 | need better work | |
| Geography | 62 | 78 | 67 | good, but could be better | |
| Mathematics | | | | | |
| Science | | | | | |
| Typewriting | | | 38 | Weak | |
| Shorthand | | | 74 | poor | |
| Arithmetic and Accounts | 38 | 45 | 48 | | |
| Woodwork | | | | | |
| Engineering Workshop Practice | | | | | |
| Engineering Drawing | | | | | |
| Physical Training | | | | | |
| Arts/Crafts | | 60 | 4 | good but unsatisfactory | |

No. of times absent ........ 13

Remarks: Joan has the ability to do much better work, she must make up her mind to concentrate & improve in both performance nature, this is property date.

Next Term begins ........ 13th April, 1953.

Teacher in charge—Secondary Department

Principal

The Parent is requested to sign the Report and return it on the first day of the new Term.

---

## WALSALL EDUCATION COMMITTEE.

### Junior School.

# REPORT for Half-year ending December 1948

Name of Pupil: Joan

Form: 4th Year B ........ No. in Form 47 ........ Position in Form

| SUBJECT | MAX. MARKS | MARKS AWARDED | FORM TEACHER'S REMARKS |
|---|---|---|---|
| ENGLISH: | | | |
| Reading | 20 | 20 | Very good |
| Composition | 20 | 20 | Very good |
| Language | 20 | 16 | |
| HISTORY | 20 | 10 | |
| GEOGRAPHY | 20 | 10 | |
| NATURE STUDY | 20 | 16 | |
| MENTAL ARITHMETIC | 40 | 5 | Very weak |
| ARITHMETIC | 20 | 13 | Careless mistakes |
| PRACTICAL GEOMETRY | 10 | 7 | |
| ART | 20 | 20 | Very good |
| HANDICRAFTS (Boys) | | | |
| NEEDLEWORK (Girls) | 20 | 16 | |
| Religious Instruction | 20 | 14 | |
| **TOTAL** | **250** | **168** | |

Conduct: Talks too much

Attendance: Very good

General Observations: Joan is capable of a much better result

Form Teacher.
Head Teacher.

Parent's Signature:

*School Reports 1949 & 1953*

# PART TWO

# WOMANHOOD

## CHAPTER TWENTY-FIVE

# First Job.

My first job was in a large electrical components factory situated on the outskirts of Walsall town. I had been employed as an office junior and filing clerk, with the promise that I would be given a shorthand-typing job as soon as a vacancy occurred.

The clothes in which I started work caused me a great deal of embarrassment, consisting of old school uniform skirt, cardigan and shirt. The cardigan was darned at the elbows and the skirt was too small, revealing knobbly bare knees when the current fashion was for mid-calf-length hems. My feet were bigger than my sisters', and I had bunions so I wore a pair of mum's down-at-heel court shoes that slothered as I walked.

My agreed wage was Two Pounds per week and take home pay One Pound Sixteen Shillings and Eight Pence. Of this I had to give mum thirty shillings for my keep and use the rest for paying my bus fares to and from work; and keep myself in clothing and make-up. Unable to afford canteen meals, mum packed me up sandwiches and often these consisted only of bread and butter and a packet of crisps.

I sat at a bench in a large office, filing part-notes listing components into small drawers. Typists and ledger clerks worked in the same office, and the Head of Department sat in solitary splendour in a glassed-in corner of the room. Filing was monotonous and boring. Eyes and head ached with peering at the seven-figure number typed in the right hand corner, and predictably my mind wandered and notes were wrongly filed. Fear of getting the sack haunted me, knowing as I did that filing clerks were ten-a-penny. It was almost impossible to get another job without a good reference.

My sanity was saved, once an hour, on the hour, when it was my job to pick up the tray of Internal Memos and distribute them around the various office and factory Departments. The fingers of the clock moved maddeningly slowly as I watched for the hour hand to register. I dashed pell-mell along the corridors, in and out of the offices, rushing to win a few extra moments at places of interest.

Outwardly confident and cheeky I soon made friends here and there. In the Drawing Office my friend Big Bernie would lift me effortlessly onto his drawing board, then laugh uproariously at my efforts to get down again. Down from the offices and into the bowels of the factory I ran, weaving my way through clattering machinery to where some of my former school fellows worked on an assembly line. They too did repetitive jobs, fitting identical small screws into identical sockets, but they weren't bored. They sang and laughed as they worked, joking with each other and shouting insults to passing factory hands.

They earned a lot more money than I did and I envied them this and their happy working conditions. Dad overheard me say to Margaret that I wanted to ask for a transfer to the factory and declared that no daughter of his would be a factory worker; I would have to leave Shelley Road immediately. His snobbish attitude in this direction has proved to be one of the few things I have to thank him for.

All around the huge factory I sped delivering memos to Storemen and Patternmakers, Furnaces and Fitting Shops. I loved the way the older mens' faces lit up when I ran into their Departments, bringing with me, so they said, a breath of fresh air. I found it surprisingly easy to form friendships with such men, assuming as I did that their interest was purely avuncular.

Women, on the whole, I found prickly and petty-minded and I only felt at ease with elderly ladies who tended to 'mother' me. I often confided in them about the difficulties of my home life, being a natural chatterbox with a desperate need to be understood. One older lady, who lived alone, offered me a home. She was warm, round and cuddly and I dreamed of her adopting me, and of me pouring out my pent-up love on her in return. But dad, who had been telling me to 'get out' since I was thirteen or so, said that I was under sixteen and couldn't leave home. If I did he would have me put into Care. The kind lady retired shortly afterwards and I lost touch with her.

The office where I worked was large, housing about twenty people, the men sitting at long desks at the top half of the office, the women at the lower end. I had not yet heard of segregation and accepted this as normal and right. Some of the staff had been there thirty years, sitting at the same desk, writing entries into identical ledgers. How did they bear it, I wondered, trapped like birds in cages away from the green earth and fresh air? Year after boring year. But they seemed happy enough and were tolerant of my youthful exuberance and clowning.

The Boss of our Department, Mr. Bullow, was a tall, skeletal, dour, dried-up husk of a man. He sat behind his glass partition watching us like a bird of prey. To be summoned to his presence was a common dread among young and old alike. After six months I could bear the filing job no longer. Summoning up my courage I knocked, trembling, at his door. He bade me enter, looking at me over his bi-focals in a distasteful manner.

'Yes, girl, what is it?' He tapped his pen impatiently on his ledger. Hands held tightly behind my back to stop them trembling, heart hammering against my rib-cage, mouth dry, my voice came out high and wavering.

'Please, Mmm. Mmm. Mr. Bbb Bullow, mmmmmay I speak to you a mmmmoment?' Stuttering was another of my afflictions when I was under stress. My hands shook so badly at such times that I had great difficulty in controlling them at all. Mr. Bullow sighed impatiently.

'Come on, get on with it girl. I haven't got all day'.

'Ppplease mmmay I mmmove off Part Notes, Sir? I'm losing my typing speed'.

'Sit down, Miss .....What's yer name.?'

'Stafford, Sir, Joan Stafford'.

'Sit down Miss Stafford. I've been meaning to have a word with you'. His cold fish eyes looked unfeelingly at me, making me feel like an unsavoury specimen under a microscope. Oh no. Not the sack. Dad would kill me. After what seemed an eternity he continued to speak.

'You are a bright girl, Miss, but a careless worker. Misfiling Part Notes causes serious inconvenience in this Department. And your Time-Card shows slackness in this direction, too'. (Yes, I thought, and so would yours if you had to help get kids out to school and run the gauntlet of our dad in the mornings.) He had removed his glasses and was twirling them slowly in his bony fingers. His false teeth were like rows of china cups, much too large for his shrivelled mouth and causing his speech to be punctuated by high-pitched whistles. With his hooked nose and bald head surrounded by a wispy, moth-eaten fringe, he reminded me of an ancient eagle.

Office gossip had it that Mr. Bullow had not married until late in life, to a woman much younger than himself, and that they had produced a quiver-full of children. (Fancy waking up and finding him next to you. Or worse, making love to you. Ugh. . . .). I beamed nervously at him and said I was sorry for mis-filing but I was bored. I would try to concentrate harder if put onto typing.

My smile seemed to touch and thaw some tiny part of him, and his mouth twitched at the corners.

'Miss Stafford' his voice was less severe now. 'It is against my better judgement, but nevertheless you may start Invoice Typing on Monday. I trust that you will spend far more time applying yourself to your work and less time entertaining the men in the Department. Do I make myself clear?'

'Yes, Sir, of course, Sir. I promise, Sir. Oh, thank you, Sir'. I could even have kissed him— on the cheek of course. I raced to the bottom of the office and imparted the good news to the Invoice typists, grinning like a Cheshire Cat.

'Oh well' observed old Mavis, head of the typists, 'there won't be a dull moment with you around'. Not if I could help it there wouldn't be.

Looking back I realise I had a real talent to amuse at a very superficial level. I used it as a tool for survival, to camouflage my almost pathological sensitivity, sensing rightly that people wouldn't understand. The staff ribbed me about the serious autobiographies I read at break-time, the only outward clue to my being 'different'.

In the Invoice Department, typing endless boring invoices, I learned of many things from the gossiping that went on around me. The 'girls' were grannies, mothers, spinsters, one single unmarried mother, and one bride-to-be. They discussed, without reservation, their relatives, sex lives, abortions, illnesses, fears and phobias. Earthy Black Country girls, they pulled no punches and spared me no blushes. Here was laid the cornerstone of my adult education in Life. I came to that office a raw, unschooled, naive girl and left just two years later, infinitely wiser.

My second and final interview with Mr. Bullow led to my handing in my Notice. No pay rise had been forthcoming, as promised, and I still had no decent clothes to wear. My father had also stated that my board money would be increased and it was up to me to ask for a rise. I entered the office with great nervousness, but had learned to control myself better.

'Please, Sir, my father says I've to ask for a rise, now I've been here two years'. The Boss didn't even look up from his ledger.

'You may ask, Miss Stafford, but you will not get. . . .'

It was time to move on, to move up. I would let nothing keep me from bettering myself. I applied for a job as a Secretary in a Bit and Stirrup Manufacturers, near the railway behind Shelley Road. I borrowed decent clothes from Margaret and literally charmed my way through the interview. I lied about my shorthand-typing speeds, assuring myself that I would soon catch up, having an excellent memory and a quick brain. Armed with these tools I would somehow rise above Shelley Road. Salary was agreed at Three Pounds per week and I would also save on bus fares. The Upward Journey had begun.

## CHAPTER TWENTY-SIX

# Our House–circa 1954.

The Council painted the outside of our houses every few years, using mud-brown and bottle green alternately. Internally, our house had never known a lick of paint since it was built; now twenty years on, peeling plaster and chipped paintwork assaulted the eye from every angle.

To be fair dad did make a small effort at decorating around this time, but he soon gave up. One weekend, armed with an old sock and a tin of dirty cream paint that the council workmen had left behind some years before, he set to work on the living room. His plan was to stipple the dirty green walls with an interesting pattern, but he gave up the unequal task after completing most of one wall. Nothing daunted he then declared war on the bathroom in a similarly original fashion, and with as little success. Armed with another tin similarly inherited, of old white emulsion this time, and a bicycle pump, he began to spray the flaking-plaster walls. This method, though spectacular, was also doomed to failure, and the wall and concrete floor were left unbecomingly streaked with emulsion. Later I papered it myself and managed to persuade a boy-friend to box-in the iron bath.

Just after his demob dad flirted briefly with carpentry. He might have had more sucess had he bought some proper tools and wood for the job. Paying for anything, however, was strictly against his principles. (With, of course, the exception of alcohol.) Out of a couple of tea-chests, one afternoon, he fashioned a small chair and bookcase for the boys' bedroom. Having no knowledge or patience for joints and dowelling, he simply used nails. Still in use when I left home, being the only furniture in my brothers' bedroom besides the bed, the bookcase spent its entire life leaning drunkenly against a wall. The chair seat was set at a cruel angle that dug deep into one's thighs, so it was used only to drape the boys' clothes over when they went to bed. No wardrobes ever graced the bedrooms at Shelley Road. But then, wardrobes would have been redundant as only dad had more than one complete set of clothes.

During the thirty years my parents lived at Shelley Road no electric wall-plugs were installed. The wireless ran off the hall light socket and consequently there was no light on the stairway. Luckily for us there were plenty of street lights around.

During the twenty years I lived there mother never owned a washing machine. After the boiler in the kitchen was dismantled she was left only with the bath, and a zinc pot in which to boil whites on the gas stove. From the age of about thirteen I was regularly kept off school, to help with the Monday Wash and Tuesday Ironing. This involved bending over the bath at an uncomfortable angle, scrubbing collars and cuffs with Sunlight soap. After washing and rinsing shirts and dresses were dipped in a bucket of Robin Starch. A Reckitts Blue Bag was swirled about in the starch to add extra brightness to the wash. Everything must be wrung out by hand and then fed through the rollers of the ancient mangle, before being hung on the clothes lines in the back yard. I recall how often these lines snapped, the washing falling on the sooty yard. All must be rewashed and starched. What tears of anger and frustration I felt at such times.

Only flat irons were in use until I left home, heated on the gas stove and gripped with pads of singed rags. The 'ironing board' was the kitchen or living room table, padded with an army blanket. The ironing took most of Tuesday. Cleanliness was before Godliness in Shelley Road and I vowed that, when I grew up, I would never do the washing on Monday, nor waste my time ironing. With the advent of synthetic materials I have been able to keep both those vows.

Living so close to the Potteries crockery was very cheap, and pretty 'seconds' could be purchased from the market for pennies. Mum had no money to spare for such luxuries and we were often reduced to drinking tea out of jam jars. Cups were cheap white crock, still in use after the handles had been knocked off and only relegated to the dustbin when they no longer held tea. We never owned a milk jug. There were a few chipped and cracked white plates, a couple of tin plates, and on many occasions we were reduced to eating out of dad's old army Mess Tins.

Cutlery consisted of bent forks, a few cheap tarnished knives, and an assortment of tin spoons. When all seven of us sat down together there was not enough cutlery to go round. When handles came off knives they just continued to be used without them.

The sheets given to mother during the war by the W.V.S. were still in use, sewn side-to-middle long ago and now frayed beyond repair. Finally she gave up the unequal task of sewing the rips and we three girls totally refused to perform this chore. If dad would not give money for such necessities then the sheets must just drop to bits.

The living room suite was a mess of torn cushions, with wooden arms sticking out of the brown upholstery. It was re-covered in Nineteen Fifty-Two (on Hire Purchase of course). The only piece of lino in the whole house was in the living room. It was wine coloured with a black key pattern, and polishing this until it shone like glass was a chore I hated. Dad had obtained this lino free from one of the offices he had worked at. Mum had pegged her last hearth rug some years before and the scrappy rug before the fire had long since lost its pristine freshness and colour.

There was an old sideboard in the living room, and a bureau. The bureau was a piece of reproduction furniture, initially bought on Hire Purchase by dad, but payments as always being kept up by mum and so paid for out of the housekeeping. It was father's pride and joy. He kept it locked and carried the key with him.

This, then, was the house occupied by the Stafford family circa Nineteen Fifty-Four. As we children matured we grew more quarrelsome, cramped, overcrowded and frustrated. Only the Babby remained gentle and kind. The least bright of us five children, he had by far the nicest nature. My youngest brother was now ten and already as tall as Keith. He loved his mom, and from the earliest age sought to protect her and help her wherever possible. As we older children spent more and more time away from the house the Babby became the main target for dad's abuse. Dad jeered at him unmercifully, cruelly chiding him about his poor scholastic performance and making cutting, hurtful remarks about the Babby's clumsiness and halting speech.

My father delighted in telling his youngest son what a 'knock-kneed, non-intellectual, scatter-brained, nit-wit-numb-scull' he was. This was a favourite expression of dad's. There were many others that memory has mercifully obliterated.

After being convicted of fraud, dad had to take more lowly jobs before charming his way back into a position of trust. During his years in the job wilderness bitterness ate into him, and he now dedicated himself totally to the task of crushing our spirits and driving us from home. He probably drank more, now, to forget his own hopeless situation, but I will always remember those dreadful years that have 'no place in time'. How he hid himself skilfully at the crook of the dark staircase, to gleefully leap out at an apprehensively ascending child. How he whispered obscenities as he passed me in the house, or pushed me as I passed him on the stairs, laughing gaily when I lost my balance and hurt myself. How he kicked my beloved cat just for the pleasure of hearing me scream. As the cat thudded against the wall he would say, in his mocking voice.

'Oh dear, Joan. That careless pussycat's fallen off the mat again'.

How he hurt me when he punched Keith, or taunted him and the Babby until they cried for mercy. Tears of theirs, tears of mine, tears of mum's. She would finally scream for dad to. . .

'Stop. Stop it. Stop tormenting 'em, Leave 'em alone. Oh, please leave 'em alone. . .' There was no escape for any of us. Not yet.

Margaret could always get the better of dad now in a verbal argument, so he left her alone. Josy, too, was a match for him, kicking him deliberately and viciously on his bad left leg where she knew he had phlebitis. He now ignored Josy, turning the full force of his cowardly bullying onto us younger and less able ones.

My sisters left home shortly afterwards, Margaret to marry and Josy to live with her until her own early marriage. It was now up to me to protect mother and the boys. I did my best, only slightly handicapped by the fact that I was a total mental and physical coward.

## CHAPTER TWENTY-SEVEN

# First Love, Paul.

May, Nineteen Fifty-Four. At lunchtime the staff from the factory where I worked migrated to the huge park across the road. One of the Black Country's beauty spots, The Arboretum was Walsall's proudest possession, a sparkling jewel among the sooty factory chimneys and teeming slums. Like the Common and the canal it, too, had played a part in my childhood, being a place of tranquil beauty that fed my spirit. Covering about three miles of rolling pasture, it was a magic place for both child and adult. As children we had dipped our feet in the paddling pool, rocked on the see-saw, and soared on the swings. We had braved the dizzy heights of the helter-skelter and clung grimly to the giant-strider.

The play area was set well apart from the rest of the park, linked by a tree-lined avenue edged with aviaries, where peacocks spread their brilliant feathers. Here were cooing doves and flitting songbirds, brightly coloured parrots and one malevolent, moulting eagle. The wooded slopes above the aviaries had hidden generations of lovers, cradling them in its leafy dells and hollows. Here were meandering, shaded paths and tiny stone bridges spanning the trickling brooks that fed the lake.

Surrounded by huge overhanging Weeping Willows, fringed by great Bulrushes, the huge expanse of water supported families of gliding swans and ducks. A pretty mock-Victorian boat-house overlooked the lake and from here could be hired rowing boats. Beside this lake I lay one May lunchtime, slightly apart from the raucous office girls. The close-cropped grass was starred with fallen cherry blossom, scenting the air. Before me the Willows trailed their delicate branches in the glistening water and young birds sang in the soaring branches above me. Munching an egg sandwich, library book open on the grass before me, I rejoined Percy Bysshe Shelley in Italy.

A splash of oars on the lake directly in front of me caused me to look up from my book, and my eyes met Paul's. I see him now, across more than thirty years, and time has not dimmed the memory. Sunlight caught burnished golden hair and his handsome sunburned face was sprinkled with tiny freckles. He had a generous wide smile and beautiful even teeth. Strong tanned arms rested on the oars, and I could tell that he was tall. He wore a sky-blue shirt with sleeves rolled up to the elbows, and the jacket of his grey pin-striped suit lay neatly beside him. A book lay open on his knees. All around him were points of sunlight bouncing off the water, shimmering up and down the sides of the boat, dappling him with light.

The eyes that met mine were sherry-brown and full of laughter. Shock-waves swept through my body, causing me to blush and avert my eyes.

'Good afternoon, My Lady of the Willows'. His voice was almost accentless and slightly mocking. I pretended to ignore him, burying my blushing face in my book. I heard him step out of the boat and pull it onto the shore, before sitting down about a yard distant from me. The office girls began to giggle and cat-call.

'Hey, Joanny, Wot yow got what we ain't got?'

'Hey, Joanny. Can we share 'im. Don't be greedy. Gee us a bit'.

I was ashamed of their crudeness, ashamed of my shabby clothing. I could sense his magnetic presence, sense his gaze upon my face. I wanted to run away. . . . from what? Hide away. . . . from what? But I was trapped, ensnared by this man's strong physical presence and my own emerging sensuality.

'Joanny. A lovely name for a lovely young lady. May I see what you are reading? Ah, the bold Shelley. Do you know him well?' He lay back on the grass, squinting against the sunlight, arms behind his leonine head. Slowly he recited from memory. . . .

"When the lamp is shattered, the light in the dust lies dead. . . ." and I joined in to show off my own knowledge. The ice was broken and we were soon chatting animatedly, all shyness forgotten. Paul was eighteen and worked in Local Government in Walsall. Grammar School educated, his family had been too poor to enable him to go on to University to read Classics, as he had wished.

Too soon it was time to go. The girls moved away. We stood up and Paul towered above me, telling me how much he had enjoyed my company and asking if he could meet me after work. The meeting was arranged. The wheels of destiny had begun to turn.

Back in the office the hours ticked leadenly by. How very long are the moments between lovers' meetings; precious, wasted moments, wasting youth and joy and life. How quickly pass the hours when lovers meet. And so it was with us, that night, and all the other days and nights in the months ahead, made sweeter by the knowledge that soon Paul would join the Army for two years as a National Serviceman. All the beauty and heartache of young love was encompassed in that blessed time, when the world was young.

Paul was a loving, affectionate bear of a man and he adored me. Snuggled in his arms I drank deeply of his love, hungrily feeding my famished body, desperately trying to find a sort of security. Hand in hand we strolled the leafy lanes together, or sat beside the still canal. In fields of corn, hidden from prying eyes, we lay together, tempting the Fates with our desperate longing for fulfilment. Again and again I fought him off, terrified of pregnancy, horrified at all that that implied. Never, never would I be trapped as my mother had been.

Summer turned to autumn. Paul wrapped me around with his overcoat and pledged himself to keep the chill winds off me for the rest of his life. Lying on beds of fallen leaves he taught me scraps of Greek Mythology and the names of the stars, and together we declaimed snatches of our beloved poets. Winter came, and we played like children in the snow, building snowmen and pelting each other with snowballs. We simply never felt the cold when we were together.

CHAPTER TWENTY-EIGHT

# Memories of Paul.

Since the end of the Second World War male conscription into one of the Armed Forces was obligatory. Youths were required, at the age of eighteen, to serve two years National Service, or work for two years down the mines. There were few exceptions to this rule, although a term of deferrment could be sought in the case where family hardship, at the loss of a wage, could be proved. Paul was sitting vital Civil Service Exams when I met him and had been granted a few months deferrment. It was this knowledge, the certainty that soon we would be parted, that made our time together so sweet and precious.

He insisted on taking me home to meet his family, proudly wanting to show me off to his parents. His father welcomed me with open arms. I was to find that fathers usually did. He had been a Steel-worker and had suffered a severe spinal injury in the course of his work. Unemployable for some years, receiving only a small disability pension, he turned his capable hands to anything in order to feed his family. Well-read, he had high ambitions for his children, determined that they would have a better chance than himself.

Paul's mother was equally strong-minded. Of stout peasant stock she was proud of her physical strength, going out charring to enable her children to stay on at school and take vital exams. At home her house ran like clock-work. I sensed from the first meeting that his mother did not like me, regarding me with deep suspicion. This, too, was to become a familiar pattern in the future.

Their home was shabby but cosy, and I soon felt at ease

despite Paul's mother's coldness. On winter evenings I joined the family around the piano, our numbers sometimes swelled by numerous aunts and uncles, for a sing-song. Here I learned to love the old songs that Paul sang unselfconsciously to his fifteen year old sweetheart such as '. . Silver Threads among the Gold . . .' and . . . 'When your hair has turned to silver, I will love you just the same', or 'When you were sweet Sixteen'.

The music on such evenings had wonderful variety. 'White Horse Inn' would be followed by 'Kathleen' and perhaps a Chopin Piano Solo by his sister Marie. Then Paul would serenade me with 'Babyface, you've got the cutest little babyface . . .'. I wanted, on such evenings, for time to stop, desperately longing to stay forever in this world of laughter, song and family warmth. Yet always a part of me stood aside, watching myself joining in their jokes yet weeping somewhere inside, lost, alone, afraid.

With Paul's arm around me on the sofa, on some such evenings, we listened to the gramophone playing 'Il Trovatore', 'Pagliacci', Brahms, . . . classical music of which I was almost entirely ignorant. The haunting strains of Grieg's 'In the Hall of the Mountain King' will always transport me to that time, that place, seeing Paul leap up to change the record, wind up the gramophone and carefully change the needle.

On such winter evenings Paul and I sped back to Shelley Road, about two miles distant, on his bicycle. Sitting side-saddle on the cross-bar, his strong arms enfolding me, I leaned back onto his chest and listened to his serenade.

'The girl that I marry, a girl I can carry will be. . . .'

'Rose Marie . . . .'

'When you are in love, it's the loveliest night of the year. . . .'

'People will say we're in love . . . .'

'Beautiful dreamer, Queen of my song, list while I woo thee with soft melody. . .'

Paul knew them all . . . and sang only for me. As I became familiar with the words I added my song, too. The wind tore through my thin clothes, caught at my bare legs, tried to snatch away our love songs. We felt no pain. Not now, not yet.

So many memories of Paul to warm me in my old age. Do the young still love as we did? I do hope so. One wet winter's night we ventured to the bright lights of Birmingham. We felt worldly and grown-up as we explored the coffee bars of the big city. And in the centre of New Street Paul literally stopped the traffic with his joyful interpretation of Gene Kelly's 'Singing in the Rain'. Regardless of the pouring rain bouncing off his bare head and soaking his suit he danced in and out of puddles, on and off the pavement, weaving around lamp-posts.

"I'm singing in the rain, Just singing in the rain.
What a glorious feeling I'm happy again. . . ."

A crowd gathered. I shrank with embarrassment and almost burst with pride as he serenaded me, then bowed his head like a true professional to the spontaneous applause.

Anywhere, at any time, he would catch me up in his arms and twirl me round and round.

'Paul, stop it! People are LOOKING! Behave.. PUT ME DOWN!' He was larger than life. . . . vibrant, whole. And he would soon leave me. Anyway, he had to leave me every night at Shelley Road. As we clung together near the garden gate, saying our 'Goodnights' – (I snug inside Paul's overcoat, nestling against the warmth of his body), dad would sometimes pass us wordlessly on his way from the pub. It would have been wiser to have been in bed when dad came home but young lovers are not known for their caution. It was so hard to leave Paul's embrace a moment sooner than was necessary. I had told him something of my history but sensed that he thought I was exaggerating.

'Come on Jo-Jo, let me meet him. He'll be O.K. All fathers worry about their daughters and think no young man's good enough for them. . . .' He didn't understand, nobody did.

'No, Paul. You'll only make it worse. You must never call at our house, ever'.

From where we stood I could see my parents' bedroom, and on 'good' nights the light would go on quickly and the danger passed. But most nights dad waited up for me, for the pleasure of showering me with filthy accusations and dark threats, mum sitting at the fire, mute, helpless, wringing her hands, rocking. On and on went his voice, his evil tongue searching for mental chinks in my fragile armour. His current nick-name for me was 'BOWG', which he gleefully interpreted as 'Body On Waste Ground', insisting that this would be the natural culmination of my nocturnal wanderings.

Huddled miserably in my bed, fingers pressed to my ears, I could hear his voice droning on and on. Sometimes, standing outside the shut bedroom door, twisting the handle very gently, he repeated over and over again, softly, evilly.

'I'll kill you soon. Kill you. Kill you. You're just filth, filth, filth. . . .' Twenty years later I had still not banished that voice, waking up from nightmares screaming 'Stop. Stop. . . . please STOP. . . .'

It was Christmas time when Paul accidentally met my father. On Christmas morning I had opened the gifts that Paul had left for me, together with a boxed card containing a satin heart pierced by an exquisite diamanté brooch, in the shape of a Lover's Knot. Inside the card he had printed the words of our favourite song.

"Sweetheart roses, sweetheart roses, led me to your door.

And in the garden of my heart, they'll bloom for ever more. . . ."

A tree had been put up by Keith and myself, and a few trimmings. Keith had had great fun decorating dad's latest acquisitions, two stuffed stags' heads. Moth-eaten and mounted on large wooden shields, they had been 'rescued' from the Mess where he often drank and now adorned the living room walls. Keith had stuffed tinsel up their noses and dribbled it out of their mouths. Mum hadn't noticed but dad would soon do so.

Dad was out at the pub and my two brothers and I chatting companionably, when there was a knock at the door. Keith answered it and led Paul into the house. In two days time I knew he was due to start his six weeks Basic Training at Oswestry Barracks.

His startled glance took in the stag heads, the shabby

room, and mum weeping quietly by the fire. Good manners coming to the fore he approached my mother, handing her a box of chocolates.

'I'm so pleased to meet you, Mrs Stafford. How do you do?'

Shame engulfed me. Shame at our house. Shame at mum's clothes. Shame at mum sitting wringing her hands, tears pouring down her cheeks. The boys saved the situation, asking Paul about his army posting, and they were soon chatting away like old friends. Mum's voice reached me from far away.

'Joan' she whispered hoarsely. 'Joan. Yer dad'll be in in a minute. Yer know wot 'e's like. . . . quick. Get 'im out quick..'

Too late. Dad was home. Paul stood up from the battered sofa and extended a welcoming hand.

'How do you do, Mr. Stafford. . . .' Dad brushed past Paul's hand and sat down in his usual chair, totally ignoring him. He got out his newspaper and began to read. The clock ticked, the dog scratched. The boys had vanished out of the front door as dad entered in at the back. I stood transfixed near the door into the kitchen, desperately willing Paul to escape with me to the clean outside world. Paul tried to engage mum in conversation but to no avail. . . . minutes ticked by like hours. After an eternity father spoke without lifting his eyes from his newspaper.

'I wish to have my meal. You. . . . what-ever-your-name is– please observe there is a door leading to the kitchen, which connects with the outside of this house. Use it'.

Paul rose and faced my father, or rather towered above him, fists clenched at his sides, anger burning his cheeks.

'Certainly. But would you mind giving me a reason?' Fathers' words were equally measured.

'This is my home and I will not tolerate uninvited rabble. Get out and take 'it' with you..' he concluded, nodding his head peremptorily in my direction. I fled and Paul joined me on the back porch, folding me inside his overcoat, pressing me to him to try to stop my trembling.

'The bastard. The bloody bastard. . .' His tears mingled

with my own.

'I'm so sorry. . . . So sorry. I didn't believe you love. You can't stay here. Not when I'm away. I'll ask mother if you can have my room. You'll be sixteen soon. We could get married and maybe I'll sign on and we'll get an army house. . .'

But I knew I must not escape from Shelley Road into marriage. Instinctively I knew I would only be exchanging one trap for another and my spirit longed to soar free. I needed Paul's love so desperately. I needed my freedom even more.

## CHAPTER TWENTY-NINE

# Lost Virginity. 1955.

My sixteenth birthday coincided with Paul's completion of six weeks Basic Training. Six weeks, for me, of monotonous employment and the undiluted misery of Shelley Road. Paul's daily love letters were my only link with my sweetheart, the only bright spot in the day.

With his usual enthusiasm Paul had thrown himself totally into his new life and was well on the way to earning his first stripe. I occupied myself by writing long letters, pouring out my sense of loss and longing. Proudly I wore his spare Royal Artillery cap-badge on my lapel and counted the hours until our reunion.

No young girl would have been seen dead in spectacles in those days, so I groped my way blindly to Birmingham's New Street Station to meet Paul. I was late from having caught a wrong bus and embarrassed by having just mistakenly entered a Gentlemen's Toilet, much to the amusement of the male occupants. Knowing I couldn't possibly find Paul, I waited at the end of the platform away from the jostling crowd, pretending to read the time-table.

Without warning I was swung high into the air, Paul's beloved, beaming face below mine, eager lips seeking mine. For long moments we clung together, speechless, his rough khaki battledress jacket prickling my blushing cheeks. Then, swinging his kit-bag effortlessly onto his broad shoulder, other arm around my waist, we made our way to the bus stop.

Seated on the bus speeding us to Paul's home and a family reunion, my eyes searched his face for signs of change. His cheeks were ruddy and he seemed to have grown, some-

151

how. His black beret was tucked jauntily into his epaulette, his burnished hair close-cropped. His whole confident being brightened the dull February day. I felt comforted and warmed.

Always desperately insecure and lacking confidence, I felt shabby and unworthy of Paul, acutely conscious of the glaring faults in my own dress. I was teaching myself dress-making, handicapped by lack of pattern or good scissors. Patience was not one of my virtues and the hem of the lilac circular skirt dipped here and there for lack of fine stitching. Margaret had loaned me a white blouse, a size too small, the button-holes straining across my bosom. A small boater was perched upon my head, hand-covered with the same material as my skirt and sporting a trailing white ribbon. The whole outfit was marred by my shabby top-coat and the black canvas 'pumps' on my feet. Paul didn't seem to notice or mind, but I did. Very much.

Standing back from Paul's welcoming family I had time to observe the main change in Paul that I had tried not to acknowledge. His voice was louder, bragging even, and he sprinkled his conversation liberally with coarse army expressions such as 'bull-shit' and 'jankers'. His father had got in a few bottles of beer for Paul's homecoming and I watched with growing fear his obvious beer-drinking ability. There was something about his mannerisms and speech that reminded me of my father, and chill fingers of apprehension clutched at my heart.

Paul's mother had made me a birthday cake. As I blew out the candles Paul told me I must make a silent wish, and I wished that Paul, my Paul, would be there when I opened my eyes. He wasn't and never would be. His present to me was a marcasite ring, and to please him I let him place it on my left-hand fourth finger.

That evening he had arranged to meet another 'squaddie', a new army 'mate', at Walsall Town Hall. Here, every Saturday, a dance was held, complete with a band and resident singer. We were to make up a foursome with his mate and girl-friend. I had never been to a dance before and felt sick with shyness and fear.

Inside the Town Hall, introductions made, Paul and

Jackie made a beeline for the bar, leaving us girls to trail behind them making desultory conversation. Ethel was 'common', a factory girl with scarlet lips, matching finger-nails, and a knowing air. A Woodbine dangled from her lips and she drank gin, laughing loudly and squinting through the smoke.

Jackie and Paul were having a great time reliving their exploits on the assault course and mimicking their Sergeant-Major. I had asked Paul for an orange juice but he had laughed and told me not to be a baby, handing me an orange juice spiked with a large gin. Ethel winked knowingly at me and said something about 'Mother's ruin'. I tried to look worldly, sipping my drink, an unfamiliar Woodbine between my fingers. Both gin and cigarette tasted dreadful but I persevered and in a short while was laughing gaily, too, shyness and self-consciousness evaporating.

Finally, at about nine-thirty, the men staggered from the bar and lurched with us onto the dance floor. Paul held me very close, uncomfortably close, and his breath smelled of stale beer and cigarettes. Ethel and Jackie drifted past us, their lips locked in a passionate kiss. Paul leered drunkenly at them and said he knew what Jackie would be getting shortly lucky devil. I tried to look as if I hadn't heard.

On the way back to Shelley Road Paul suggested we take a short-cut through a derelict churchyard. I tried to argue, being more familiar with the road, but he insisted. It was after midnight, I was tired and cold, and Paul knew I was terrified of the dark. Beside the ruins of the church he left me alone whilst he staggered behind a tomb-stone and noisily made water. Then silence. Long minutes passed. Frantically I called out 'Paul. Paul. Where are you. . . . Paul . . . don't tease. . . .' Still he did not reappear.. 'Paul. Paul. . . .' I was sobbing now. Suddenly he scooped me up from behind and carried me into the porch of the church, laughing. He pressed me against the wall, kissing me savagely, hands groping my body.

'No. Paul. Oh please. . . . Paul. . . . stop'.

I fought with every ounce of my strength, scratching and tearing at his face and hands. He forced me to the ground, pinning my six stone body beneath his thirteen stone of muscle and sinew. I screamed as he tore his way into my unconsenting body. Soon it was over. Rape. Intercourse without consent. I was sixteen years old that day and no longer Jail Bait. I felt dirty, cheated, contaminated, violated, unutterably sad. The walk home was a nightmare.

Dad had locked me out but Keith came down to let me in.

'What's up our Jo? What ya crying for?' He noticed my torn clothes and mud-covered coat.

'Did ya fall down? Cum 'ere. Let's 'ave a look at ya'. Staying in the kitchen away from the bright light, I assured him I was O.K. That I'd just fallen down outside.

'Go to bed Keith. You've got to be up early in the morning'.

Locked in the bathroom I washed my bloody knickers. The mirror above the sink reflected my tired face, tear-stained and mud-streaked. I looked like a broken doll. Tears of self pity welled anew and I sobbed quietly for my 'Mommy'. But I knew she couldn't help. She was lost, too. Betrayed by men.

Huddled under the bedclothes, clutching my sock-covered hot-water bottle between my thighs, I made a decision. If I were pregnant I would kill myself. The thought somehow comforted me. I felt so tired, too tired to fight any more. In the darkness I took off Paul's ring and threw it across the room. After he had violated me he had said 'Now you belong to me. I love you'. He was wrong on both counts. I belonged only to myself and always would. And I knew that what had just happened was in no way connected with love.

I continued to meet Paul while he was on leave, and to write lovingly to him when he returned to Barracks; but from now on I would keep him at arms length, on 'a string'. I kept him like this for seven long years, along with many other men. Finally, to escape the torment of being near me, he threw up his career with the Civil Service and went abroad.

During Nineteen Seventy-Seven, on a brief return to Walsall, I was dining in a restaurant in Birmingham with a lawyer friend. There was some sort of celebration going on at the next table. Watching discreetly behind my dark, prescription-lens glasses, I gathered that one of the two adolescent girls with the party was celebrating a birthday. She was just 16 years old. As I watched the girl shyly cutting the cake, I became aware of something familiar about the face of her doting father. It was Paul. Stockier, hair slightly greying but still, quite recognisably, Paul. He caught my eye and I raised my glass, removing my dark spectacles to see if he recognised me. Swiftly he came over to our table, beaming his beautiful broad smile.

'Jo. Jo Stafford. How are you? You haven't changed a bit'. I introduced him to my friend and he sat for a few minutes at our table, while we tried to cover twenty or more years. He talked so proudly of his two daughters, how well they were doing at school, insisting on introducing them to me. We were just leaving, so I crossed with Paul to their table and shook hands with them. Then I spoke a few words to the eldest.

'Sixteen years old? I was just your age when I knew your daddy'. She was just a child, a little girl, and she knew her daddy would watch out for her. No one would be allowed to take advantage of his beloved daughter. I dared not look into Paul's eyes as I turned to go, lest my eyes betray my feelings.

CHAPTER THIRTY

# Goodbye Paul.

Paul returned to Barracks, leaving me alone to worry lest I were pregant. I had periods irregularly anyway, so for weeks my mind knew no rest, waking or sleeping.

Finally, one beautiful day, my period arrived. I felt as if I had been given my life back again. On my way to work I noticed the first real signs of spring. Everywhere was bright and fresh, and in this mood of thanksgiving I decorated the living room in Shelley Road. At lunch-time I rushed down to the market and bought rolls of cheap wallpaper. I had told the girls in the office I had tummy ache and might not be back in the afternoon. Mum was startled to see me, and even more startled when I set to with paste and wallpaper.

'Yer dad'll goo mad, Joan. Yer know what 'e's like'.

'I'm sick of living in a slum. Nobody else's bothered, so I'll just have to. I'll have it done before dad comes home, don't worry'.

I borrowed a wallpapering brush and scissors from next door and set to work, getting mum to perform the tedious task of cutting the trim off the rolls. I worked instinctively, making a reasonable job of it, having a tremendous sense of achievement when I'd finished.

Dad never said a word to me about it, but mum said he was amazed at my handiwork. Over the next year I redecorated the whole of Shelley Road and laid a tiled floor in the kitchen. It meant going without a lot of things myself, but it was worth it. With cheap material off the market I hand-sewed curtains and bedspread for my own room, tying the curtains back with pretty silk ribbons.

Paul's letters still arrived daily, full of love and plans for the future. My own letters were sporadic, as I was far too busy flirting with a lad in the next office who took me boating on the lake at lunch-time, and I went with him to the pictures to see 'Seven Brides for Seven Brothers'. The young girls in the office were scandalised at my 'two-timing' Paul.

'You'll get yerself a bad name, you wait and see'.

I had changed my job, increasing my pocket money by one pound, so I could afford to take myself out and be slightly better dressed.

There was a small dance-hall in the centre of Walsall called the Mayfair. It was the 'in' place to go dancing and I knew Josy and her fiancé often went on a Saturday night. I also knew that it was frequented by lots of Servicemen. I was determined to go.

Early one Saturday morning I went to Walsall market and bought five yards of soft fine white poplin, scattered with tiny red hearts. Back home I spent the rest of the day designing and sewing the dress I would wear that evening.

I had bought a bottle of hair-lightener which turned my dark blonde/brown hair a golden colour. Curling tongs were wielded haphazardly but reasonably effectively. No debutante going to her first ball would have taken greater pains over her dress and make-up than did I. Over and over again I scrubbed my face and reapplied Pond's Cold Cream, before dusting my nose with face powder. A touch of lipstick was used for rouge, eyelids smudged with blue creme, eyebrows sketched in with black pencil. Daringly I drew a bold black line right around my eyes. Teeth were scrubbed, and bright lipstick drawn in a cupid's bow on my mouth. A liberal splash of 'Californian Poppy' perfume and I was ready. It was a pity I couldn't afford stockings and only had cheap shoes to wear. Luckily we didn't own a full-length mirror. What I could see looked good.

Dad's weekend routine was generally predictable and consequently he was easily avoided. He usually came in from the pub at three and went to bed, rising again at six-thirty or seven. I heard him now, moving heavily about upstairs. Mum was bustling about the kitchen, getting him a cup of tea. I didn't want her to see me all dressed up, knowing she told dad everything. It would only give him more ammunition to fire at me.

When I heard her going upstairs with the tea I crept through the kitchen and out of the house. I felt like a real lady as I walked down Shelley Road, head in air, feeling the soft generous folds of dress brushing my ankles. The little children I still occasionally looked after ran up to me, admiring my dress.

'Can I cum wiv ya, Auntie Jo' pleaded my favourite four-year-old, shoving her grubby hand into mine. I bent to kiss her golden curls.

'Not today, Linda. It's your bedtime. I promise to take you a walk tomorrow'. She knew I never broke my promises and ran happily back to her game. As I turned the corner of Shelley Road two women neighbours were walking towards me, laden with shopping. As I passed them I heard one say.

'Bugger me, Doris, 'er looks like a bloody Red Indian'. That is how I learned to be more sparing with rouge. Angrily I rubbed my burning cheeks with the back of my hand, wishing that I had a hand-mirror.

Waiting at the terminus for the bus I was assailed by stomach cramps. I had forgotten to eat and I knew that a combination of hunger and nerves caused the pain. I was used to this pain by now and determined not to let it stop me enjoying myself. Out of my handbag I took a packet of five Woodbines and a box of matches. Lighting a cigarette was very difficult because of my constantly trembling hands, but I was learning how to hold my right wrist with my left hand to keep it steady, while I lit my cigarette. I improved on this technique when in company, idly playing with an unlit cigarette until some kind man dashed forward with a light.

Ascending the stairs of the bus on a windy day, wearing a circular skirt, was an operation fraught with peril. It was not just good manners that made the men already at the bus stop insist that I go first. Head held high, bottom tucked well in, back ram-rod straight, right hand clutching the hand-rail and the left hand, with handbag, weighting the dress behind. In a howling gale skirts still billowed out and up, but one just continued in a stately fashion, stonyfaced and deaf to wolf-whistles.

No queen ever received better training in assumed dignity than I. If a strange man sat beside me and tried to engage me in conversation, I just stared out of the window, entirely unheeding. Or read a book. Being 'picked up' by a man in that way, no matter how handsome or cultured, was 'common'. My nick-name around Shelley Road soon became 'Lady Muck'. They were just jealous.

Courage almost deserted me at the Mayfair, I walked past the doors a few times before making myself ascend the stairs to the upper hall. 'Look well if Josy isn't here won't it? Look well if no one asks me to dance! Look well if I've forgotton HOW to dance!.

I paid my two shillings and entered the ballroom. The gramophone in the corner was playing 'Your Cheating Heart', and I briefly felt guilty as I thought of Paul. It soon passed.

## CHAPTER THIRTY-ONE

# A Dance in Time.

The Mayfair was not as large as the Town Hall, and much more romantic. All around the dance-floor were alcoves lit by soft pink lights, where non-dancers stood both singly and in groups. A mirrored many faceted globe rotated above the dance floor, dappling the dancers with shifting drops of light. The theme music from 'Limelight' filled the air and young couples danced slowly around the room 'smooching', holding each other very close, barely moving their feet in time to the music.

In the cloakroom I recognised two of the girls from the factory where I had once worked.

'You'm ever so brave cumin' 'ere on yer own, ain't 'er, Jean?' Jean, dressed in a garish sugar-pink dress and matching dangling ear-rings was squinting before the mirror, applying a liberal coat of mascara.

'Oo, arr. Ain't ya gorra mate ta cum wiv? Yow can cum wiv us next wik, if ya loike. Can't 'er Rita?' I pretended to be friendly, but these girls were far too common for me to associate with, now. They would be bad for my image.

'Don't wait for me girls. I'll be simply ages doing my hair. I'll look for you when I've finished'. I knew, as soon as they were out of ear-shot, that they would tell each other what a snooty la-di-da bitch I was. I sat for ages in the cloakroom, adjusting my frock, recombing my hair. The pain in my tummy was much worse.

I tagged behind a crowd of girls as they moved out of the cloakroom and into the ballroom, standing almost hidden behind them under the nearest arch. A crowd of South Staffordshire soldiers was standing a few feet away, and after a few minutes one of them moved towards me.

'Hello. I hope you don't mind me asking you, but are you

related to Josy Stafford? I used to go to school with her. I saw you come in and thought you were Josy for a moment, but of course you're taller than her'.

He introduced himself as Cedric and I immediately recognised his name. He had been a prefect at Josy's school. It seemed that all the Grammar School boys had been in love with Josy.

'Take your partners, please, for a Quickstep', boomed the M.C., and Cedric asked me if I would dance with him. I stuttered and tried to explain I was not sure I could dance, but he assured me he wasn't much of a dancer either, so we could 'kick each other to death' or learn together. As 'Love is a Many Splendoured Thing' bathed us with music, we stepped onto the dance floor and into a friendship that spanned thirty years.

Cedric was not tall, perhaps about five feet nine. His father had been Indian and he had inherited his fine, aquiline nose and high cheekbones. His hair was black and straight, his skin palely brown. He had dark, intelligent, serious eyes and small even white teeth. On the arm of his uniform he sported Corporal's stripes, despite having been in the army only a short time. He was nineteen, and had obtained deferrment before being compelled to do National Service, because of his mother's dependence on his pay. His father had long ago deserted the family, leaving his wife to bring up three boys. After Grammar School Cedric had worked in an office, but he had plans to better himself when he got back to 'civvy street'. In the meantime he was determined to use his army service to maximum advantage.

I felt so safe and secure in his arms, sensing instinctively that he could be trusted. Courteous, considerate and gentlemanly, he was a stimulating knowledgeable companion, possessing a subtle but uproarious sense of humour. We were soon laughing and joking like old friends.

We danced every dance with each other. Nat 'King' Cole warbled the current hit song 'A Blossom Fell. . . .'. As we circled under the flashing globe in the 'Last Waltz', I felt wildly happy, safe in Cedric's arms. I wished I could stay there forever. . . .

My new partner insisted on taking me back to Shelley

Road, which meant him missing the last bus back to Barracks. He would have to walk or hitch the twenty odd miles to Lichfield, no distance at all, apparently, to a man newly in love. We stood together by our garden wall, just around the corner so dad wouldn't see us when he walked up the road. It was so easy to talk to this gentle man, already wise beyond his years. Underneath the street lamp we stood, smoking Woodbines and getting to know each other. The night was cold so we were soon sharing Cedric's greatcoat. Before he left me he gave me such a gentle, loving kiss. A kiss that almost wiped out the memory of Paul's savagery. Many years later, in memory of that girl and that moment, Town Councillor Cedric led a children's protest march from that very spot.

From that night on we spent every possible moment together. Cedric had applied to serve with the Forces abroad and knew he could get his marching orders at any moment.

For the remainder of the summer, Cedric carefully healed the wound that Paul had left, and although there was a strong physical attraction he did no more than kiss. Gradually I ceased to be afraid and began to relax in the warmth of his embrace. He had a very strong moral code, stoutly insisting that I was young and vulnerable, and as such must be protected.

With little money to spend we walked the leafy lanes, or occasionally went to the pictures. I recall, at this time, seeing 'The Student Prince' with the beautiful Anne Blythe. Cedric and I rarely actually saw much of any film as we both needed glasses for long distance, and these obstacles got in the way when we kissed, which was frequently. Best of all I recall our walks back to Shelley Road, tarrying in our favourite doorways for the many cuddles we enjoyed so much.

We also spent a lot of time in coffee bars, listening to the Juke Box and meeting other soldiers and their girl-friends. Espresso coffee was a recent invention, and bamboo-bedecked coffee bars had recently sprouted up all over the country. Teddy Boys were everywhere, with their long Edwardian jackets, drainpipe trousers and brothel-creepers. My brother Keith dressed in this fashion and I was horrified. I wouldn't have been seen dead with a Teddy Boy, considering them 'low class'. Many were the clashes between Teddy Boys and Servicemen after the pubs closed on a Saturday night.

Some weekends Cedric had to do Barrack Duty, and on such weekends I travelled by bus to Whittington Barracks. There were miles of lovely woodland around the camp, where we wandered hand in hand. Sometimes Cedric would persuade one of the Naafi workers to make us up a picnic of sandwiches and cakes, and we would find a leafy dell for our leisurely meal.

How clearly I recall such a day. It was nearly autumn and the canopy of leaves overhead glistened in greens and golds. Speckles of sunlight sprinkled the grass and early-fallen leaves cushioned our reclining bodies. It was a very hot airless day and I wore only a thin cotton dress and pants. Cedric had taken off his battle-dress jacket and tie and opened his shirt. We had finished our repast, and lay back in the long grass contentedly. Some comment of mine caused Cedric to throw back his head and roar with laughter. I started to tickle him, and we rolled over and over, like two young puppies playing innocent games. Suddenly, without warning, everything changed. Cedric was on top of me, kissing me passionately and urgently, roughly exploring my body with urgent hands. I did not resist, did not want to resist, wanting to be very close to him, to be part of him.

With a mighty effort of will he pulled himself free from me, pulling my dress decently down over my legs. Breathing heavily, he gazed at me for a long moment, his eyes speaking to me with a mixture of longing and compassion. Then, gently, he stroked my hair, pushing it back from my forehead in the loving gesture I was now so familiar with. His touch now was reverent, like a father with an errant child. Leaning back on his elbow, calmer now, he searched in his battle-dress pocket for two cigarettes, lighting them both and placing one to my lips. The danger was past, for the moment. Finally he spoke.

'No, my little Jezebel. It's no good. I'm responsible for you. Someone has to be. You need to be free to grow, to spread your wings, to enjoy being young. When I get back to Blighty I'll marry you, if you'll have me. . . .' Out of his pocket he drew a piece of paper and handed it to me.

'There it is, darling. I didn't tell you before. Didn't want to spoil the picnic'. The papers instructed him that he was being drafted to Cyprus in late September, to join the peace-keeping force already there, to be shot at with real bullets. His voice continued, as if from far away.

'Promise me only one thing, love. Promise you'll write to me as often as possible, and that you'll never send me a 'Dear John'. Just wait until I get back before you tell me it's all over between us. . . .' I promised.

The last week of his Embarkation Leave coincided with the Autumn Illuminations at The Arboretum. Miles of brilliantly-coloured fairy-lights decked the autumn-tinted trees, mirrored in the lake. Painted wooden swans, softly illumined, rested on the island in the centre of the lake. Amongst the tree-tops soared hardboard doves and moons. The quaint bridges over the many small streams were lit beneath their pretty stone arches, and here and there in the leafy 'Lion's Den', where lovers trysted, were elfin grottos, secretive and magical.

Cedric and I clung to each other on his last night in England, hidden in the 'Lion's Den', looking down upon the shimmering scene beneath. From the Pavilion floated the haunting sound of the 'Intermezzo' from 'Cavalleria Rusticana'. We had sat in this same spot every night for a week, listening to the same music and enjoying the sweet kisses that grew sweeter as the hours sped inexorably by.

Just before we left the park for the bus station, on that last night, my sweetheart handed me a gift. It was a necklace with delicately faceted blue stones that reflected the lights. I have it still, more treasured than any gold ring or diamond I have since received. That necklace represented months of saving and self-sacrifice for Cedric, and I knew it was given to me in true, abiding love.

We parted at Walsall Bus Station. A Juke Box from a nearby café blared out the popular song 'Auf Wieder-sehen'. . . . it was almost too much.

"We'll kiss again, like this again. Don't let the tear drops start.
With love that's true, I'll wait for you.
Auf Wiedersehen, sweetheart".

Without even looking into Cedric's beloved eyes I asked him to go. . . . NOW.

'Just turn and walk away. Don't wait. You know I hate goodbyes..' He immediately responded to the tone in my voice, turned on his heel and quickly marched away into the night.

Blinded by tears I staggered upstairs on the bus, then just in time glimpsed my father halfway down the aisle. I went back downstairs and right to the front of the bus where no one would see my distress. I sat with eyes closed, made myself breathe deeply; willed the tears not to fall. Not yet. I recalled an expression in French that I had discovered recently in a book. 'Tout passe'. I repeated the words over and over again in my head like a Mantra. 'Everything passes'. It didn't help the pain one bit but it gave my mind something to do.

I raced off the bus before it had properly stopped, and was away along the dark streets before dad had even alighted. When I got home mum was sitting by the fire, trying to poke some life into it in readiness for dad's expected arrival. She looked at me, then spoke conspiratorially.

'There's a bit of dinner for ya in the oven. Don't let ya dad see it. Tek it up ta bed with ya. . . . wot's up, our Joan. 'Ave ya bin cryin?' Quickly I told her that Cedric had gone. He had often visited the house when dad wasn't there, and I had had the feeling that she liked him. Seeking words of comfort, mouth working soundlessly for a moment with the effort, she finally spoke these words.

'Don't cry, our Joan. Daddy says soldiers don't cry. An' anyroad, you'm better off without that lad, yer know. If ya'd 'ave married 'im yer'd only 'ave 'ad black babbies'. Even in my misery, my mind registered the astounding fact that my mother had just attempted to give me, possibly for the first time, some real motherly advice.

I rushed up to bed before dad entered the back door. The tears could flow now. My friend, my trusted companion, my sweetheart, would soon be thousands of miles away. I felt I would never be able to bear this crushing weight of loneliness and loss.

CHAPTER THIRTY-TWO

# Second Job.

I stayed at my second job for six months, learning a great deal about bits, stirrups and other horse furniture. The Foundry was situated at the back of Shelley Road, facing the railway and Sewage Farm. At lunchtime, if I didn't want to go home, I could sit in the field opposite the factory and read a book.

Two elderly, very aristocratic gentlemen owned the Foundry, kind fatherly men with exquisite olde-world manners. They were patient of my initial slowness with shorthand, observant of my nervousness, and did all they could to put me at my ease. I quickly regained my typing speed by using only two fingers, rather than attempting to touch-type as I had been taught.

Once a month there was a Board Meeting attended by the other directors. It was my job to polish the long table in the Board Room and arrange pads of blotting paper, pens and ink at each appointed place. I asked permission to pick and arrange a bunch of wild flowers from the field as a centre-piece and 'my' gentlemen were pleased to let me. At the Board Meetings I took my first Minutes and began to feel like a real secretary. My shorthand would never be very good but my excellent memory stood me in good stead, and soon I developed my own unique brand of shorthand.

My tasks were varied. Filing, letter-writing, typing invoices, running errands in the Foundry, and making the tea in true office junior fashion. There were only two other women employed in the office and I got on well with both of them. Ena was the part-time Invoice clerk, a pleasant married woman of about twenty-seven. Grace was an ancient spinster, maybe nearly forty, with iron grey hair; given to sporting sensible tweeds and brogues. She was the Book-keeper and Telephonist and had been at the Foundry since she left school. Grace seemed friendly, but like most female Heads of Department I was to encounter, somewhat officious and with an uncertain temper.

For six months all went well. I got to know most of the Foundry workers, both men and women, soon becoming familiar with the joys and sorrows of their personal lives. Open and friendly by nature, a natural chatterbox, these people opened up to me easily and soon became friends.

When Cedric was on leave before he went to Cyprus, he would meet me at lunch-time and we would walk hand-in-hand across the field, to sit by the wooden bridge spanning the river. These months were among the most settled and peaceful of my life. They would soon end.

One Monday morning I arrived at the office two hours late, having arranged with one of the Bosses the previous Friday for time off to visit the dentist. Chattering happily as usual I took off my coat and sat down at my typewriter, beginning to tell of my visit to the dentist. Suddenly Grace rounded on me, face blazing with anger, fists clenched at her sides.

'Why did you not ask MY permission for time off?' I stuttered that I didn't know I had to. It had never happened before. . . .

She marched to the Boss's office and rapped angrily on the door. Bidden to enter, she slammed the door behind her and I could hear her raised voice saying that I was insolent, and that either I was dismissed from my job or she would leave forthwith. NOW. Shocked and trembling with fear I was summoned before my two kind gentlemen. They were very, very sorry. They could not possibly lose Grace. They assured me they would give me a good reference and two weeks extra wages, in lieu of Notice, as Grace had refused to work with me in the office. It was still THE SACK. I collected my cards from Grace and left the Foundry.

Not daring to go home I caught the bus into Walsall and went straight to the Labour Exchange, mind in a turmoil. Dad would throw me out if I could not pay my Board

Money. Where would I live? How would I survive? Margaret must also be paid her Club money weekly. Now married to a joiner, just having had her first baby, she would be unable to help me out. For some time she had earned pin money by running a Mail Order Catalogue, from which I chose items of clothing and was slowly building up my wardrobe. I paid her five shillings a week.

I knew, from newspapers and the length of the dole-queue I now stood in, that unemployment was rife, especially for young people like myself without paper qualifications. Standing in the queue at the Employment Exchange I was filled with horror, still sick and shaken as I was by my sudden turn of fortune.

Finally I was summoned to a sordid shabby cubicle littered with dog-ends. A totally uninterested woman took my particulars, then scanned her list for suitable vacancies. The only job available was for a Lawyer's clerk in the centre of Walsall, but they wanted someone with experience in Law and preferably over twenty. She looked at me coldly and said to come back next week. Gathering every ounce of courage I asked for the name of the firm-PLEASE- as I knew someone whom it might suit. Reluctantly she told me. 'Marlowe & Malpass'.

I raced down to their offices right in the centre of Walsall, before my courage deserted me. At the Reception Desk I explained that I had been sent from the Labour Exchange about a vacancy. Could I see the person concerned, please? An internal call was made and I was told Mr. Malpass would see me after the next client left, in about fifteen minutes.

Mr. Malpass was another fatherly gentleman. I got the job on a month's trial.

## CHAPTER THIRTY-THREE

# Lawyer's Clerk.

Lawyers were notoriously mean regarding wages, and one of the reasons I was given this job was that I would require less salary than a twenty-year old. I had dared to ask for Three pounds and ten shillings per week, an increase of ten shillings above my previous earnings.

Mr. Malpass was a self-made man, having worked his way up from office boy to Senior Managing Clerk. One son, Mr Kenneth, was a qualified lawyer practising with this firm; another son, Mr. John, was an Articled Clerk. My Boss had grown daughters of his own and treated me in a fatherly fashion. A big bear of a man with large, bad teeth, he perpetually wore a black serge three-piece suit, a heavy gold watch-chain spanning his ample midriff. His accent was pure Walsall.

Referring to me always simply as 'Miss', he was patient of my many mistakes as I hurried to learn the strange legal language and complicated office procedure. I shared an office with just one other girl, Pearl, who was Mr. Kenneth's secretary, a spinster in her early thirties. She was a bit prickly but we rubbed along together reasonably well, and she was patient in instructing me how to type up Divorce or Injury Briefs for Counsel, House Conveyances, Leases, etc, or how to fill in forms when people died intestate.

Pearl it was who introduced me to the dark secrets of the Strong Room, a 'must' for all new staff members. A dreadful, fascinating initiation into the legal world. A combination-locked heavy steel door led into a small room, shelved all around from floor to ceiling. Upon these shelves reposed thousands of bulky Cases tied neatly around with legal red tape. Almost one hundred years accumulation of Murders, acrimoniously-dissolved Partnerships, bitterly-contested Divorces, Paternity Suits, Inheritance Disputes, neighbours' Quarrels, Injury and Insurance Claims, Last Wills and Testaments. The whole of life in all its complexities; a feast for a compulsive curious reader like myself, to be dipped into at random when I could skive away from my typewriter.

My cheeky confidence was very superficial and I despaired of learning, in one short month, the myriad tasks I must perform as a Lawyer's clerk, having yet to realise that I did possess a high degree of native intelligence. I still thought of myself as rather stupid, and that when I did succeed in mastering a complex task it was a fluke. I confided in Mr. Kenneth that I hated my given name of Joan and he kindly drew up a Deed. I could now legally call myself Joanne. It seemed important at the time.

The month passed – and I was kept on. It was hard work but rarely boring. There were plenty of other young people downstairs in the main office with whom to strike up a friendship. There was much joking amongst us, plenty of scope for youthful high spirits, at least when Miss Holmes was not in ear-shot. Forty years, girl and woman, she had served Marlowe & Malpass, giving up her youth to look after aged invalid parents. Now, lonely and embittered, the sound of our youthful laughter annoyed and angered her. Luckily she worked alone as a Book-keeper, in a separate office, and was relatively easily avoided by me working as I did upstairs.

The fifteen years old office boy was the butt of many of our pranks and jokes, being very innocent and still 'wet behind the ears'. He had only just left school, without qualifications, and I was shocked to learn that he earned the same wage as myself. The battle for sexual equality was still far in the future and we just accepted these things as unfair but unavoidable.

On the same floor as my office, separated by only a window, was the Articled Clerks' Office. Three very personable young men worked there, giving me plenty of scope for flirting which came as naturally to me as breathing. Cedric was abroad, I had a semi-serious boy-friend named Michael, and I saw nothing wrong with 'Keeping my options open' – a favourite legal term.

At lunch-time we adjourned to the Clover Milk Bar along the road from the office, the 'in' meeting place for Walsall's young office set. Dining only on coffee and cream buns, we laughed and joked and listened to the Juke Box. The singers of the day were Ruby Murrey . . . ('Let me go Lover . . .') Frankie Laine, David Whitfield, Lita Roza, Dickie Valentine, Alma Cogan. . . . We knew all the words of the current hit songs, just as the youngsters do today.

Michael worked as a journalist in the newspaper office opposite the Milk Bar, joining the crowd there most days. I had met him at the Mayfair after Cedric's departure, and we were inseparable in a fraternal sort of way. Exempt from National Service because of a heart condition, he was one of the few civvy-street nineteen year old men around Walsall. Tall, emaciatedly slim, with straight dark brown hair and clipped moustache, he deliberately cultivated a 'spiv' image, much to his mother's horror. A natural showman, he was great fun to be with, and he liked hugging and kissing me, so supplying my physical needs.

Michael lived with his parents and elder sister in a large stone house on Mellish Road. He would pick me up from work in his Morris Minor Series E and we spent the evenings with his family. For over a year their house was like a second home to me, so enabling me to spend less and less time at Shelley Road.

Michael's was a popular family and their house was 'Liberty Hall' for their many friends and relatives. Mother was, as mothers always were, wary of me, but she knew her darling only son adored me, and wisely did not try to separate us. Father was older than his wife. He was retired now and able to devote much time to his piano playing around Walsall's Clubs. He was gentle, kind and considerate – and I worshipped him.

Every other weekend in the summer the family threw a party, Michael's mother making mounds of cakes and sandwiches, and guests bringing bottles of drink. Bottle parties such as this were all the rage and often lasted all night. There was little drunkenness but plenty of merry-making. Born with a high tolerance to alcohol I soon learned how to use it reasonably wisely.

Father played the piano and led the singing, thumping out 'Green Door', the current hit song, with what I soon learned was syncopated rhythm. He too was a showman and could play jazz or popular music according to his guests' requests.

It was all innocent fun. Well, nearly. During the course of the evening we usually played a game of 'Murder'. Each member of the party apart from the two people chosen to be 'Detectives' was secretly dealt a card, one of which was the Ace of Spades. Whoever drew this card was the 'Murderer'. Leaving the 'Detectives' in the living room, we all dispersed throughout the darkened house, accompanied by much giggling and laughter, and hid ourselves. The 'Murderer' must choose a 'Victim' and make himself known by putting his hands around the person's throat, whereupon the victim must give a loud scream to summon the 'Detectives'.

We would then all gather in the living room for questioning about our movements, upon our honour to tell the truth. Only the 'Murderer' could lie. It was all rather exciting and hilarious and much fun was had by all. Except me. Again and again the married men 'Murderers' chose me for a victim, using the excuse to fondle and paw me in the darkness. I was by now pretty skilled in fighting men off.

Their wives were very wary of me, following their husbands even to the lavatory if I were not in the room.

I often stayed overnight at Michael's, sleeping in a sweet smelling bed in a pretty room. I always felt, deep down, alone, but in this way I could at least have a taste of what a 'real' family was like, by proxy as it were.

In the summertime Michael and I set out to tour Cornwall and Devon despite his mother's dark forebodings about her son's well-being. We slept in the car and, I recall, dined mostly on fresh crusty rolls and creamy Devon butter. On the many unspoiled beaches we played like children in the sand, building sand-castles, playing ball games, leaping the white-horses. Hand in hand we explored the ruins of Tintagel, the alleged seat of Arthur's Round Table. It was a golden time as, like brother and sister, we played our innocent games, both vastly entertained by each other's humour. We were both too scared of the consequences to have a deeper physical relationship, playing at being in love without any real commitment. We were simply growing up together.

That Christmas, just before my eighteenth birthday, Cedric came home from Cyprus. He arrived unexpectedly at Shelley Road, straight from the transit plane. His latest letters lay unopened in my bedroom. The Babby cycled over to Michael's to break the news to me, and ran me back on the cross-bar of his bike.

In the back-kitchen of Shelley Road, without preamble, I told Cedric of my friendship with Michael– the fun I was having–how I didn't want to be tied down to a serious courtship. He was devastated, but thanked me politely for not sending him a 'Dear John'. He begged me to accept the presents he had in his kit-bag. A pair of pale blue Oriental slippers, matching dressing-gown beautifully embroidered, and a musical box that played 'La Paloma'. I have it on my mantelpiece as I write.

I agreed to meet him occasionally in the future– to 'give him a chance'. It was the least I could do. I admired and respected him very much but there was no future in our relationship. He was a poor office boy. There was no way I was prepared to settle for a drab, penny-pinching marriage to a half-caste. Together we attended one of the many Music Halls still in existence and I danced with him frequently at the Mayfair or the Town Hall. But my constant flirting with other men distressed him and soon we stopped seeing each other. Shortly afterwards he married a local girl.

How could I know that his M.E.N.S.A. brain would take him into the law and politics? Fifteen years later I looked him up, having followed his career with interest from a very long distance. Both our marriages were in tatters and we had a brief delightful affair, giving ourselves a few more lovely memories to add to our store.

## CHAPTER THIRTY-FOUR

# Man's Best Friend.

Our beloved Dog had been with us since 1946 when dad had brought her from Barracks. She had just been a tiny playful pup then and had grown up with us, sharing our joys and sorrows. Each year she had given birth to nine or ten puppies, no matter how diligently we tried to keep her indoors when she was on heat. With five children coming and going she always managed to escape somehow.

But now Dog was tired, almost blind and had a weak heart. She had been mum's constant companion during the long years of her chosen imprisonment in Shelley Road. Now it was nearing the time for our faithful friend to leave us. Each day Dog moved more slowly, only going out into the back garden when nature called. The Babby and I wept together, prayed together, brought home tempting morsels to encourage her to eat and grow strong again. To no avail.

One gloomy Saturday Dog suffered a stroke, paralysing her back legs. Tenderly we lifted her out into the garden every few hours. Indoors I knelt beside her, desperately trying to massage some life into her limbs, mum and the Babby sobbing at my side.

I sent the Babby to fetch Michael with his car, and when dad came in from the pub told him that Michael was taking Dog to be put to sleep at the Vet's. Subdued for once he agreed to go with Michael, as it would need two people to carry her from the car. Dad loved that Dog more than anything in the world. She was his link with his war-time sweetheart, and had accompanied him on many walks to countryside pubs at weekends.

Only people who really love animals can understand the

grief we felt, and I only know for myself that no death since has caused me more pain.

Much later we heard the car stop at the gate and dad's slow, heavy footsteps coming down the path. He walked into the living room holding Dog's empty collar, tears streaming down his face. He went straight upstairs to the bedroom. For hours we could hear his deep shuddering sobs.

On Monday I had to return to work. Fearful of leaving mum alone, I had agreed that the Babby should stay off school for a few days. He needed to do so anyway. He was heart-broken. We all were. I dragged myself around the office, trying to concentrate on the tasks in hand, wiping away endless unbidden tears.

Well-meaning people said, 'For goodness sake, pull yourself together. It's only a dog'. Only a dog? She had represented all that was clean and good at Shelley Road. She had been my childhood comfort and confidante, bringing solace and affection to my loveless life. She, alone, had never betrayed my trust.

For months afterwards mum barely moved from the hearth, rocking silently backwards and forwards, crying endlessly. Each lunch-time the Babby rushed home from school, increasingly fearful of finding her with her head in the gas oven or simply gassed sitting in her chair. Having no sense of smell herself, we often found her in a gas-filled house, a gas tap turned on on the unlit stove. Again and again she maintained the light had 'blown out'. But in her rare moments of exhausted hysteria, when dad had been particularly sadistic, she had often screamed that she 'would be better off dead'. I loved her but was powerless to help her.

In those days attempted suicide was a criminal offence and mental treatment barbaric and primitive. Mental hospitals were locked, barred, gruesome places staffed mainly by starched, steely Amazons who appeared to have been trained at Auschwitz. We knew of people incarcerated at Burntwood some fifteen miles away, and we didn't want our mother to end up there. So much ignorance surrounded mental illness, contaminating the whole family with its sinister threat of inherited sickness.

There were very few 'attempted' suicides, which in our enlightened age is recognised as a cry for help. Self-inflicted death was for real. During my childhood, on our estate alone I recall two hangings, two gassings, a mother who slit her throat with the bread knife, a father who drank a bottle of bleach, and one drowning of an unmarried mother-to-be. If the victims lived they faced Court proceedings and a term in a mental hospital. The stigma stayed with that person and his or her family for life.

It was up to me to try to pull mum back from the edge. I bought her a few clothes, unskilfully home-permed her hair, and dragged her to the dentist for the removal of her stumps of teeth. Nothing worked for long until Margaret dared to leave her infant son with her while she worked, paying mother 'babysitting' money. Once more mum had to be solely responsible for a helpless child, who amply repaid her with smiles and kisses. The danger was past for the time being.

My own life was about to enter an entirely new phase. One Saturday at the Town Hall dance I had dared to ask a very tall, very shy, beautifully dressed young man for a 'Ladies Excuse Me'. I needed a new semi-permanent man in my life as Michael was often away, and on this tall chap I used every ounce of female cunning to get him to ask me out. It was hard work. I had never encountered anyone so shy before, but finally I succeeded. He asked me if I would accompany him to the cinema. Wild horses wouldn't have stopped me.

Michael was jealous and we quarrelled and parted. It was never easy to say goodbye to the men in my life. They were friends, and their families filled such a void. My fears of serious emotional involvement drove me to leave their warm arms before they caged me. Selfish, self-centred and narcissistic, I gave little into such relationships, extracting every scrap of warmth and caring from them before moving on to a new love. With each new relationship my insecurity grew more and more acute.

## CHAPTER THIRTY-FIVE

# Gentlemen Prefer Blondes.

Terence was simply another tall man, another large shoulder to cry on, another male to dry my tears and calm my fears. He was an apprentice artist with a large lithographic company in Walsall. Unlike Michael however, he was shy and serious, a silent giant of a man who tried hard to guide me in the conventional ways of his world. Terence blushed easily, stammered slightly, but I soon found that beneath this shy exterior lurked a will of iron that almost matched my own. That will, and his great artistic talent, would later take him to the pinnacle of his profession.

One fateful day, shortly after we met, he was sitting sketching me as part of his homework for Night School. Suddenly he asked me if I would have my hair bleached and offered to pay the hairdresser's bill. He showed me his sketch; my face, but with short, fluffy white-blonde hair instead of my shoulder-length mousy, golden-brown locks. Why not? Before I could change my mind Terence guided me to a hairdresser and explained his sketch to the manageress. In those days bleaches were almost pure ammonia and the procedure was very, very painful. I was to suffer it every six weeks for years to come.

That night, walking into the currently favoured public house in Walsall where Terence was waiting with a friend, I sensed every male head turn in my direction as if pulled by a magnet. Pretending not to notice I swayed on my stilettos towards my boy-friend, watching his face light up with total admiration. It was powerful stuff. Too powerful. On the surface I was now a stunning sophisticated sex-symbol. I had also taken elocution lessons to iron out the last traces of my Black Country accent, The surface image was now firmly middle-class, cultured and confident.

Who would have guessed that beneath this façade was a fearful, guilt-ridden, stupid, ugly child, isolated from all human love. Even in the most loving arms, hearing the most profound words of love, I still felt this sense of isolation. Born communicator though I was, I could not convey these feelings to anyone. In company I burned so brightly, brimmed with life and laughter, a sparkling stimulating companion. Alone in bed at Shelley Road I exhausted myself with silent sobbing, full of self-doubts, the real, messy Joanne that no-one in their right mind could love. Ever.

Terence was very proud and possessive of me. I loved him dearly, but as usual began to feel trapped as the romance became more serious. With us both working in Walsall we even saw each other at lunch-time, and were accepted everywhere as a 'couple' if not yet officially engaged. At weekends I often slept overnight at his home, and shared Sunday lunch or tea with him and his parents. They made me welcome enough, but I simply could not feel part of any family, becoming restless and ill at ease at their many close family gatherings. It was, perhaps, a form of jealousy. I blamed myself for being, simply, hard-to-please.

It was time to set my sights on the bright legal lights of Birmingham. The City offered better conditions of employment and pay. Competition for jobs was fierce and good paper qualifications were usually required. At an interview, in those days, a Black Country accent would have prevented even a well-qualified girl from getting a job with a professional firm. But now my posh accent was totally a part of me, I had the right image, good references, and plenty of cheek and charm.

I got the first job I applied for. Mr. Jonathan Livingstone-Bennett was a superbly handsome barrister in his mid-thirties. Extrovert and charming, he sat with a large silver framed photo of his wife and children smiling at him from his desk.

As well as practising law, Mr. Livingstone-Bennett also ran a small Estate Agency from his office in New Street. He would, he said, be happy to employ me as a Legal Clerk, Private Secretary and Receptionist dealing with the general public. He hoped that I would be free to do plenty of overtime, for which I would be well remunerated. It all sounded too good to be true.

I had not learned in childhood Mary Howitt's poem 'The Spider and the Fly'. Flattered by his obvious appreciation of my professional talents I happily walked into his parlour.

CHAPTER THIRTY-SIX

# Wining and Dining.

Commuting by train to Birmingham I felt grown-up at last, a real career girl. Crossing New Street at rush hour on my way to the office one brilliant spring morning, a beaming policeman held up the traffic for me to cross. Swaying sexily on high heels, feeling elegant in new lavender blouse and tight matching skirt, I felt exhilarated and content. The policeman engaged me in conversation for a moment in the centre of the road, causing a motorist to lean out of his window and shout.

'Who says a policeman's lot is not a happy one?' The ugly duckling from Shelley Road now knew, without doubt, that she had finally turned into a swan– on the outside, anyway.

My Boss was often away at Court on legal business, and I was free to organise and run the Estate Agency with just one junior typist. To the manner born I dealt with telephone calls, interviewed house-buyers and sellers, typed letters, taking it all easily upon my nineteen year old shoulders.

During the day Mr. Livingstone-Bennett would rush in and summon me to his office for dictation, patient and considerate regarding my lack of shorthand speed. His barrister friends dropped in often, on the pretext of legal business but mainly to ogle or flirt with me, openly envious in a good-humoured way 'of Johnny's sexy secretary'. Nothing I couldn't handle in an equally light-hearted manner.

My train back to Walsall left at 5.20 p.m. The office closed at 5 o'clock, leaving plenty of time to dash to the train and meet Terence for tea at the Gaumont Restaurant.

Things ran smoothly for the first few weeks as I settled into my new career. One night as I was just putting on my coat, after dismissing the office junior and locking the Estate Agency door, Mr. Livingstone-Bennett dashed out of his car.

'Miss Stafford.. so glad I've caught you. Urgent business cropped up with the 'Porter versus Porter' case. Need a new Brief drawn up before the Hearing tomorrow or I'll lose it. Do you mind awfully staying late and giving me a hand? I'll run you to Walsall so you don't need to worry about your train'.

As he dictated to me in his private office at the rear of the building, he paced the floor behind me. Again and again he would lean over, hands on my shoulders, and ask me to read back the rough Brief from my shaky shorthand. He smelled beautifully of aftershave and I noticed how carefully manicured were his nails. The strong sexuality from both of us almost tangibly filled the office.

Trying to pretend I hadn't noticed anything, when the dictation was finished I stood up to go towards my typewriter. Gently and firmly he removed my notebook from my shaking hands, laid it on the desk, and led me with a practised hand towards the walk-in Strong Room. I knew what I was doing– he was a married man– yet I allowed myself to enjoy his sweet urgent kisses with minimal resistance, until his hands wandered to my breasts. With a firm 'No' I pushed his hands away until he got the message. Kissing only was allowed.

Johnny was a big man and could easily have over-powered me, yet I knew, somehow, I was safe. I was in charge. Seduction, not rape, was his game, and I was about to enjoy every moment of it without ending up the loser.

'Call me Johnny. May I call you Joanne? My lovely, innocent Joanne you are adorable. Forgive me, I got carried away. . . .'

'Mr. Liv. . .Johnny, my boy-friend will be waiting for me in Walsall. If I type this Brief up quickly will you please be sure I'm not late for the appointment. Terence is a very jealous man'.

When Johnny's Rolls Royce pulled up in a side street at

the rear of the Gaumont, Johnny took my hand and kissed
it, murmuring gentle apologies for his boorish behaviour.
Demurely I accepted his insincere words of regret and his
kiss on the cheek.

'See you tomorrow, Joanne'.

Terence was furious at my lateness, but accepted my
excuse of overtime. I didn't tell him Johnny had given me a
lift. Terence was my security, the clean part of my life. I had
no intention of losing him.

At the office, before clients or the office junior, Johnny
treated me with studied indifference. It was a game we both
knew how to play. As a married man he was, for me,
untouchable. I had dealt with far too many Paternity cases
to have any illusions about the relationship. I knew what
Johnny wanted of me— and I knew without doubt that he
was not going to get it, but of course I never told him so. I
don't think he would have believed me, anyway. He could
have charmed the birds from the trees, but he could not
charm me into his bed.

Increasingly frustrated at his lack of success Johnny tried a
different tack, leading him into very dangerous waters
marriage-wise. He asked me to accompany him to dinner,
one evening during the week, at the Chateau Impny at
Droitwich. For me it was like being asked to attend
Buckingham Palace. The Chateau was a baronial hall-cum-
high class restaurant, frequented by the very rich Birmingham 'set'. It was often featured in the Tatler Magazine that
lay about in the waiting room at the office.

Why not? I was less worried about his wife finding out
than about Terence discovering my duplicity, but it was an
offer I couldn't resist. My hair, I decided, would need
washing more often; and Terence was informed that I
would be spending Thursday night at home for this
purpose.

Johnny and I drove up to the Chateau one early summer
evening, the Rolls crunching on the gravel. A uniformed
flunkey dashed to open my door and hand me out of the car,
then took Johnny's keys and drove the car to the rear of the
hall. The whole experience was breath-taking and I had to
resist the urge to stand like a goldfish with my mouth open.

Within were monks' benches and suits of armour, great displays of fresh flowers and huge mirrors reflecting dazzling chandeliers. This, indeed, was living.

The head waiter showed us to our table and lit the red candle in the exquisite table centre-piece. I was wearing my little black dress and Cedric's necklace, a fresh orchid given by Johnny pinned in my cleavage. Inside I trembled like jelly, terrified that I would commit some social 'gaffe'. Outwardly I was the picture of high-born sophistication.

Johnny tasted the ordered vintage wine with much ceremony, sending back at least two of the proffered bottles. Carefully he translated the French menu for me, advising me which meat to eat with the chosen wine. I chose to eat whatever Johnny was having, in order to observe which cutlery he used from the bewildering array before him. Slowly I relaxed and allowed myself to absorb my surroundings.

Johnny was on form and sparkled with charm and wit, plying me liberally with wine. Another bottle was ordered to replace the 'dead man'. The food was like a still-life painting on Sèvres plates. The only minor hiccough in the evening was caused when Johnny loudly called for the head waiter, sending his steak back to the Chef with instructions to return it 'well done' and not 'bloody raw'. I did feel he could have been more polite, and that it would have been wiser not to have drawn attention to himself quite so obviously.

I loved being treated as a lady, Johnny standing up when I re-entered the room after I had been to the 'Ladies', and seating me in my chair. This was where I wanted to belong, not Greenpark Estate.

All too soon it was over and we were driving through leafy country lanes, on a back road to Walsall. All too soon the Rolls stopped in a side-lane and Johnny took me in his arms, his ardour fired by the wine, caution thrown to the winds. But he dared not go too far without my consent and I managed to fight him off. Poor Johnny, he must have had such high hopes of that evening. How could he know that this child-like innocent was old and wise in the ways of men, and could handle drink better than an Irish Navvy.

Like many men he thought he could buy a woman; one just had to find the right price.

Over the next few months I led him on, Johnny putting himself more and more at risk as he publicly flaunted me before his friends, becoming more indiscreet as we wined and dined in the best places around the Midlands. Finally I left his employment, hurriedly, when one of his friends warned me that Johnny's wife had a private detective on her husband's trail. She was about to cite me in her divorce as soon as enough evidence was gathered. To be named as a co-respondent in an upper-class Divorce Hearing would have been death to my legal and personal ambitions. Ironic, too, for poor Johnny to have to pay such a price for such acute frustration. And I certainly didn't want to lose Terence, who I was pretty sure would not believe my tale of 'total innocence'.

## CHAPTER THIRTY-SEVEN

# Start of the Sixties.

It was a wonderful time to be young. Post-war austerity measures were gradually losing their grip, man-made fibres brought beautiful clothes within the working-girl's price range, and young screen Goddesses and Models reigned supreme. From every magazine Jean Shrimpton and Twiggy peeped out, doe-cyed tantalising childwomen, while from every other cinema hoarding Marilyn Monroe and Brigitte Bardot touted their teasing sexually provocative wares. Hairdressers worked overtime as young girls strove to emulate their particular idol, and the sales of eyeliner rocketed. Lips were pale, almost white, trained hopefully into becoming pouts.

My hairdresser used me as an occasional model for hairdressing shows, enabling me to wear my hair in the latest styles and colours weekly, without cost to my own pocket. One heady day, for a dare, I walked the length of New Street in Birmingham sporting Pink hair and matching tights. It took a lot of courage, but I was more than compensated by the attention I received. Terence encouraged me to be more daring in my dress and chose many of my clothes for me.

We were part of a Youth Cult that lasted for more than a decade, acutely conscious that we only had a few brief years to flit like brightly-coloured butterflies around the social scene. We burned the candle, unremittingly, at both ends, those of us who did not get caught in the marriage trap. My sisters, tied to kitchen sinks with small children and failing marriages, were openly envious of my life-style, but warned me darkly that I would get 'left on the shelf' if I were not careful. To be labelled a spinster was a fate worse than death or divorce. It was a Frightening Thought.

Terence bought me an Eternity Ring and talked of a 'long engagement' and 'saving for our own house'. I thought of more years to be endured at Shelley Road and knew it was not possible. Yet what was the alternative? 'Nice girls' did not have their own flats in those days, and anyway my wages would not have paid the rent. Equal pay was still many years in the future.

Terence bought himself an Austin Seven Ruby and we discovered together the lovely countryside around Wolverhampton and Bridgenorth, visiting ancient Tudor-style public houses in outlying villages. Miles of country-side lay within our reach, unfenced fields to be raced across barefoot, waist-high in Poppies and Daisies rippling in the soft winds blowing from the Welsh hills. It was a joy to be alive at such times, after being imprisoned all week in a stuffy lawyer's office.

Terence, not understanding my need for freedom, was puzzled at my uninhibited behaviour and unwillingness to be tied down to marriage. Increasingly I felt that there must be something wrong with me. We still lived in a conventional age and most people seemed to be quite content with the status quo. Since early childhood I had rebelled at constraints upon my freedom to act and think as an individual. How I wished I had been born 'like everyone else', able to easily accept marriage and motherhood.

We toured the villages of Gailey and Pattingham, Claverley, and the beautifully-named Boscobel where Charles II hid in an Oak tree. Terence fished the still waters of the canals around Staffordshire and Shropshire, whilst I sat reading or writing poems, drowsing, lulled by the hum of bees and birdsong. And on one glorious summer evening, walking in Sutton Park, Terence was both amused and embarrassed by my sudden whim to swim naked in Keepers Pool. I didn't see why not; I undressed behind a bush near the edge of the pool, where I could lower myself into the water without being seen. On another whim I decided to strike out for the island in the centre of the lake – and very nearly drowned. Terence, a non-swimmer, could only stand by helplessly while I struggled exhausted to the shore. But it was worth the danger for the thrill of feeling cold water against my bare skin and the exquisite sense of freedom I experienced. Such moments were to be treasured.

Shelley Road was a continuing nightmare. Each working morning I had to run the gauntlet of my father, himself getting ready for the office. He forbade my mother to give me breakfast, saying I did not contribute enough to the house-keeping. Sometimes she bravely smuggled me a cup of tea into the bathroom while dad wasn't looking. Through the bathroom door I could hear him taunting my young brother about his lack of scholastic ability or his round-shouldered posture. In the bathroom I would sing the latest pop-songs at the top of my voice, in an attempt to drown out dad's voice. On my way past him to the back door he would shout obscene accusations about my 'call-girl earnings' and how he knew what diseases I'd got.

I stayed out late so that dad would be in bed when I got home, the Babby creeping down to unlock the door. At weekends Terence and I partied and danced the nights away with his circle of friends. Once or twice a week I wined and dined with barristers and wealthy clients in Midland night-spots, leading an increasingly double life, determined not to miss a single chance.

Gradually I grew more experienced in dealing with ardent admirers and innocently lying to Terence about them. But by now my nervous system desperately demanded rest. I was on a merry-go-round and had no idea where it would stop.

CHAPTER THIRTY-EIGHT

# Tired Unto Death.

Having so far failed to drive me from Shelley Road, as he had Margaret, Josy and now Keith, father now stepped up his campaign, enlisting my mother's reluctant support. It was JOAN who had caused him to stay away from home more and more in the last few years, he told her, and if mum didn't get rid of me soon he would leave her. He assured her that, with me gone, he would spend more time at home. Always putty in my father's hands, worshipping him in a strange hypnotic way, she, too, now asked me to go.

Carefully I spelled out to her the obvious fact that dad would not stop at getting rid of me. It would be the Babby's turn next, and he was not yet fifteen. Also, with me gone, there would be no one left to stand up for my young brother. The Babby would work in a factory, and well I knew that my father would not easily suffer living in a house with a manual worker.

My father worked on the principle of the dripping tap, particularly with mum. On and on he droned, keeping her awake at night, painting a rosy picture of their life together or the alternative. There was a cosy bachelor flat he had his eye on in Walsall, where he, alone, would get 'peace and quiet'.

God knows I longed to leave Shelley Road, but I was terrified of living alone in the slum bed-sit area of Walsall. I was afraid of the dark, afraid of my own shadow. My nerves stretched to breaking point I would leap at the slightest sound. My nightmares, now more frequent than ever, would be unendurable. Alone. At night.

Concerned at my worsening emotional condition,

Terence talked to his parents about the possibility of bringing the marriage forward. In those days it was unthinkable to live together and his family was nothing if not conventional. Until the marriage was arranged I could perhaps stay at his parents' house.

Everything inside me rebelled at being forced into what I saw as a trap. I was not ready for marriage, knew I was emotionally messy and needed time to heal. Whichever way I looked for escape from Shelley Road I saw bars that would imprison my spirit. I had not survived all those dreadful years, endured all that poverty and misery, to be trapped now.

During the year after leaving Johnny's office I lost two good legal jobs for bad time-keeping. If I missed the train in the morning I was not five minutes but an hour, late. Extremely punctual by nature, over-anxious to please, I got up early enough. Dad got up even earlier, deliberately locking himself in the bathroom for half an hour with his newspaper. There was no toilet in there, just washbasin bath and mirror. He was not fastidious about cleanliness, rarely taking a bath or cleaning his teeth. It would have taken him five minutes to shave and he usually performed this operation in the warm kitchen.

For extra comfort he installed a chair by the sink, gleefully chuckling as I hammered on the door.

'Please, please dad. I'll miss my train'.

'Serves you bloody right. Get your own bathroom. Don't want your filthy germs in my sink'.

Another of his little tricks was to hide my one and only pair of good shoes, creeping into my room before dawn and spiriting them away. He would happily dress himself and go off to work, denying any knowledge of their where-abouts as I frantically searched the house. It was mid-day, once, before I located them in the outside shed. When I did get to work I felt exhausted before the day started, my father's sadistic laugh and filthy words haunting me as I tried to concentrate.

Mum was totally forbidden to cook for me, and the smell of dad's huge breakfast of bacon and eggs, mushrooms and tomatoes would drift tantalisingly up the stairs to my bedroom. I went to work hungry. It was worse at weekends if I had nowhere to go; I had to stay in bed until he went out to the pub at 12 o'clock. He had recently developed asthma and a serious heart condition, and some weekends he stayed home until the evening, sending the Babby to the Out Door of the local pub for eight or twelve pints of beer to 'keep him going'.

I see him now, sitting in his chair by the window, braces dangling, flabby belly protruding over his half-undone fly. His face was bloated and unhealthily flushed, a series of chins dangling from his jaw. Sitting drinking his beer he constantly burped or farted. The wireless would be on and there must be no sound to distract his listening, causing us to creep around on tip-toe, close doors without a sound, whisper only the most necessary words to each other.

He liked listening to the Goon Show, throwing his head back and roaring with laughter, exposing his discoloured teeth, tobacco stained and neglected. His small fat hands shook constantly, making the lighting of his pipe a difficult operation.

Sometimes I would lend mum money to buy the Babby shoes, or to pay the milk-man. She would plead with dad to give her extra money to repay me, trying to cajole him like a little child.

'Please, daddy. I can't manage on what you give me. I owe Joanny for the coal-man and the Babby's growed out of 'is trousers again. . . .'

'Rose, my dear. I have told you a thousand times. You must learn to manage your money better and spend less on luxuries. When you can do that I'll think of giving you more'. He wagged a fat finger at her, talking down to her like a teacher to a child.

Mother sat by the fire, chewing her lips. The shapeless slippers on her feet were her only footwear. She didn't need anything else since she never went out. Her bare legs were permanently tartan, scorched by years of sitting at the fire. Her shapeless faded dress hung in folds over her emaciated form. Her greying once-brown hair was lank and straggling. Her blue eyes were sunken in their sockets, lids swollen with constant crying.

Sometimes dad would take a thick wad of notes from the money-pocket at the waist-band of his trousers, flaunting his wealth before slowly peeling off a single pound note to throw at mother's feet.

'Come on dad. Give her some more. You've got plenty'. I once ventured, keeping the fear out of my voice. He grinned his evil grin, slowly and ceremoniously replacing the wad in his pocket and patting it.

'I would if I could, but I need it to keep my kidneys warm'.

As he drank more he became less careful about keeping our misery contained in the four walls of Shelley Road. One day, as I was walking sedately along the garden path to Terence waiting at the gate, dad opened the living room window and shouted filthy obscenities at me, using four letter words. I felt sick with shame, both for him and for myself.

As his campaign increased I was engulfed with fear and anxiety, twisting and turning like an animal in a trap. Terence was my stability, my security, and I clung to him for affection like a puppy, desperate for human contact and caring. I needed him so, but not marriage, not yet. Often I envied orphans their parentless state. In Childrens Homes, at least, any neglect was not personal and they could enter adulthood with a clean slate, ignorant of inherited knowledge.

Severe stomach pains assailed me almost constantly now as the tensions of my life increased. A tangled emotional mess inside, I felt like a tired old lady. Externally I believe I kept up the appearance of a sophisticated, carefree young girl looking quite fresh and innocent. At night, unable to sleep, I longed with all my heart for painless annihilation. I was tired unto death. At twenty.

In my short life I had travelled beyond stress, beyond pain, beyond tiredness, was standing now on the very edge of a dark, yawning abyss. My fingers were tired with clawing for hand-holds as I endlessly strove to maintain a precarious mental balance. I longed to let go, to fall, to not be. Edward Thomas's poem 'Lights Out' describes exactly this feeling.

Terence, deeply concerned, accommpanied me to our local lady doctor to see if she could help with my insomnia and trembling. As she wrote a prescription for sleeping pills she quietly advised me, knowing our family circumstances, that leaving home was my only chance. It was up to myself alone.

At work I mainly specialised in divorce in all its many aspects, most of them unbelievably sordid. I took statements daily from wives whose husbands made them perform perverted sexual acts, or beat them senseless. Grimly I typed up Counsel Briefs for Child Molestation cases or Concentration Camp Victim claims. Silent screams echoed inside my head. I felt I hurt for the whole world.

I knew many of the barristers very well, and twice I was offered sumptuous flats and money in return for my company. I wasn't offended; I just wished I had less integrity. Often I was offered financial inducements, such as freelance work with a Private Detective trailing erring husbands; to be photographed in compromising situations. The money was fabulous, the work dirty. I regretted it was not a way out for me. I knew girls who ran cars and owned flats doing just such work. I envied them their freedom and their lack of conscience.

It was a beautiful summer, but no bird song or flowering tree could lift my spirits now. The whole of life was a great Cosmic Joke, a Universal Black Comedy. No good crying to God. He didn't exist.

## CHAPTER THIRTY-NINE

# Goodbye to Shelley Road.

The fear of getting the sack haunted me, knowing that it would be very difficult to get another job with my track record. I searched the Situations Vacant column of the Birmingham Post and rang for an interview with a firm of refrigerator exporters.

Their offices were situated in a side street, deep in a slum area off Hagley Road. Dressed in a pale blue summer dress and floppy straw hat I climbed the rickety wooden stairs to the office, unsteady on my four-inch stiletto heels. My heel caught in a gap and snapped. It seemed like an omen.

One shoe on and one shoe off, I limped into the shabby office marked 'Reception'. A man sat at an untidy desk, wreathed in pipe smoke, talking on the telephone. He gestured for me to sit down. His voice was cultured and educated, deep and mature.

'Sorry about that. You must be Miss Stafford. How do you do'. His handshake was warm and firm.

'I'm Leon Barnton, Sales Manager of this Emporium. I'm afraid the Boss, Harry, has had to go out for a moment but he'll be back soon. Perhaps you'd like to tell me about yourself'.

He leaned back in his chair, feet on the desk, deliberately making me feel at ease. About forty years old, tall and well-built, prematurely balding, his twinkling sea blue eyes were kind. His nose was aquiline, his teeth perfect.

Harry Harris bustled into the office. About thirty, tall and emaciated, bursting with nervous energy, he was the original 'wide boy' even down to the Cockney accent. I was later to find out he was a superb confidence trickster–an extremely lovable rogue.

'Tell me, Miss Stafford, just for the record, why you left Johnny Livingstone-Bennett's employment. I see from your reference you only stayed with him for six months'.

I stammered that I had got tired of being chased around the office desk. He laughed uproariously and jokingly told Leon to be sure to polish up the ball and chain that their secretaries always wore. We all laughed heartily and I was given the job.

As the office was so inaccessible Leon offered to run me to and from the office each morning and evening, explaining that he lived in Wolverhampton and could easily make the five mile detour to collect me. This was wonderful news. Not only would I be earning an extra three pounds per week but I would not have to pay transport costs. I rose to leave and Leon asked me how I would manage with my shoe.

'With difficulty' was my flippant reply. Harry kindly gave Leon the rest of the afternoon off to run me home. Leon said he knew a Jewish cobbler near his flat who would fix the shoe while I waited, and if I didn't mind the mess I was welcome to a cup of coffee at his flat. I instinctively trusted him and agreed.

During the journey he told me his wife had left him some six months before, taking his little girls. He had no idea where they were, but knew his wife was accompanied by a young lover. He spoke without self-pity, but I could hear the hurt in his voice as he talked of his heart-breaking search for his children.

I learned that his father had been a Russian Jew, given to disappearing abroad for years on end. His English mother had placed him and his sister in remote Boarding Schools and had worked, as a single lady, for a large Couture House, in order to keep her family 'together'. He had had a miserable childhood before joining the army.

Music was Leon's life, playing saxophone with Traditional Jazz Bands in the evenings and at weekends. This, he knew, had led to his marriage break-up. He also worked as a freelance antique dealer in between selling jobs such as the one with Harry. He was an interesting, colourful character, an ex-army bandsman and regular soldier, having been caught up in the Second World War. It was difficult, he said, to settle to civilian living after the disruptions of those years.

His flat was high above a main street of Wolverhampton, large and rambling with huge airy rooms. Steep stairs led up from the street to the living room and kitchen, and wound on up to the two bedrooms and bathroom. Leon put the kettle on and rushed off to the cobbler's shop, leaving me to take in my surroundings. The lounge was like an Aladdin's cave, crammed with dusty china and bronzes. Duelling pistols and swords adorned the walls, and everywhere musical instruments lay about in various stages of repair. The beautiful carved Welsh dresser and mahogany Victorian pedestal table cried out for polish, and my fingers itched to set the room to rights. When Leon returned we chatted for hours, easy in each other's company. Sitting in the wing-back arm-chair I felt relaxed yet stimulated by my companion.

Our friendship developed in and out of the office, and Leon grew deeply concerned about my existence at Shelley Road. I took him indoors, at his insistence, and introduced him to my mother. Almost the same age as mum, Leon talked to her of films they had seen in their youth, gently easing her out of her shyness. She warmed to his friendliness and I knew she liked him. I confided in her about his wife and children after Leon had left.

I should have known better. She told dad. Now dad had a new weapon with which to beat me. How dare I drag his name in the gutter by being seen out with a married man old enough to be my father? He said he would tell Terence. I had already told Terence of Leon's running me home so that didn't worry me.

Next morning dad kept up a non-stop volley of abuse as I got ready for work. Ignoring him as best I could I dressed quickly, ready in plenty of time for Leon who would be waiting in his car at the gate. For some reason I dared to pour myself a cup of tea. It was scalding hot and I stood at the kitchen table sipping it, towering on my high heels above my father as he stood beside me, giving vent to his evil tongue.

What happened next seemed to take place in slow

motion. One moment I was raising the cup to my lips, the next, with a feeling of remote fascination, I found myself carefully lifting the cup above his head. Slowly, inexorably, I watched my hand pouring the hot liquid over his hair. In silent horror I saw dad's face turning puce, observing, as from a distance, how the searing brown liquid ran down his face and onto his clean white shirt. Then I picked up my bag and ran out of the back door of Shelley Road, sobbing uncontrollably, straight into Leon's arms. There was no way back.

## CHAPTER FORTY

# Epilogue.

The Swinging Sixties were only just dawning – youth only just finding its collective and individual voice. The rigid class system would be set on its head during the next decade, but until then social prejudice was still a grim reality. Permissiveness was not only frowned upon, it was positively taboo. For a man and a woman to live together outside the bonds of marriage, was to place themselves outside respectable society.

I was lucky, for once. The Jazz world that Leon belonged to was full of unconventional individuals 'doing their own thing'. No eyebrows were raised in this quarter and we were an accepted couple, welcomed into their homes and their lives.

I was, however, still on the outside – looking in. The damaged child could not easily become a whole adult; that process would take two more decades. The majority of such people, damaged in childhood, would never make it. Their solitary sentence would be for life.

Although isolated by my own inner pain and guilt, I could relate to Leon. He was my 'Daddy', lavishing on me all the affection he longed to give his lost children. And I, of course, poured out on him the dammed-up torrent of affection my own father had rejected. Our relationship was truly symbiotic, helping to heal us both.

Nature, also, was a great healing influence. Unspoiled countryside stretched from just outside Wolverhampton, to the Welsh coast. With a small tent and bare essentials we explored this huge playground each fine weekend. Living basically, close to the good earth, I began once more to glory in the scent of the wild flowers, to observe the birds and trees and babbling brooks.

Together Leon and I swam naked in deep pools hidden in hollows in the Black Mountains, or made love cradled in the swaying grass. And in the quiet of ancient ruined churches, alone, the first real stirrings of deep spirituality were heard in the silence. Hour upon hour I would sit listening . . . searching. . . . Dimly I perceived that the strange journey, from birth at Shelley Road to now, represented some sort of pligrimage. I was determined to strive to understand the reason why my particular road had been so painful.

With renewed courage and energy I faced the road ahead. Anyroad up, it was the only way.

## CHAPTER FORTY-ONE

# Summing up.

Jo Mary Stafford had now closed the door, physically, on Shelley Road, freeing herself finally by her solitary act of violence. It would be over two decades before she finally freed herself, mentally and emotionally, from that place.

How does such a damaged child become a whole adult? There is no easy answer. No Knight on a White Charger, however loving or well-intentioned, could do the job. No Psychiatrist, Psychologist, Social Worker or modern drug could help one scrap without a single-minded determination to become whole. To accept oneself, to love oneself, to find one's own place in the sun takes courage, insight, understanding, patience, experience, self-knowledge– and a whole lot of time. Perhaps, as in Jo Mary's case, a whole lot of luck, too.

The scars have to be learned to be lived with, as other people live without limbs or with dreadful illnesses. Self-pity has no place in such acceptance if life is to be lived to the full. There must be a positive wish to turn the experience around and use it– for good.

Hatred and bitterness imprison the soul. Blame and guilt, wrongly apportioned, cage the mind. Ignorance of one's own character, needs, weaknesses and strengths bars the road to future tranquility, true freedom. True harmony, real content, are only achieved by ruthlessly facing the facts, unblinkered, and coming to terms with them.

To take skeletons out of cupboards, to sit alone in their gruesome presence, to shake their hands and finally to laugh easily in their company, takes courage, real forgiveness and boundless faith in the ultimate triumph of good over evil.